WATERFOWL

WATER

Their Biology and

FOWL

Natural History

PAUL A. JOHNSGARD

Introduction by Peter Scott

UNIVERSITY OF NEBRASKA PRESS • LINCOLN

MANUFACTURED IN THE UNITED STATES OF AMERICA

Preface

OF all the books on my bookshelf, none is more dog-eared and affectionately worn than my copy of F. H. Kortright's *The Ducks, Geese, and Swans of North America*. It was this book, more than any other, that generated my interest in the biology of waterfowl and thus shaped my life. Although I still often refer to it, and especially to its superb color plates, it has become rather dated, and it is also limited in scope to North American waterfowl. Both of these disadvantages are largely corrected in the beautiful four-volume set, *The Waterfowl of the World*, by Jean Delacour, but the total cost of this set may make it unavailable to the average person. It seems to me, therefore, that there is a genuine need for a single-volume book on the waterfowl of the world, organized by topic rather than species, and stressing waterfowl biology and behavior rather than emphasizing details of plumage, anatomical measurements, distribution descriptions, or other topics of little general interest.

In addition, although the fine paintings by Peter Scott in Delacour's monograph provide an unmatched reference source, there has never been a prior attempt to bring together a series of photographs of all—or practically all—the species of living waterfowl. Assembling a collection of waterfowl photographs has been a pastime of mine for several years, and it has seemed worthwhile to extract a selection that includes as many species as possible and illustrates either characteristic plumages or representative behavior patterns. The photos included here have been selected primarily to illustrate adults of one or both sexes during typical activities or in breeding plumages. Nearly all the photos were taken personally, of captive birds for the most part. The majority were obtained at the

Wildfowl Trust in England, during the years 1959 to 1961. Were it not for that unrivaled collection of living waterfowl, the present book could not have been written, for much of my knowledge of waterfowl biology and behavior stems from the time I spent at the Wildfowl Trust during this period.

Of the 142 living species of waterfowl, I have been able to observe 136 in life, either in captivity or in the wild. Photographs of essentially all these species are included here. Of the few additional living and four extinct species for which I could not obtain photographs, I have made drawings based primarily on previously published drawings or paintings. The other drawings included in the text are nearly all based on actual photographs.

It has not been my intention to write a thoroughly documented reference text; the extensive monographs of Jean Delacour and John C. Phillips make such a task unnecessary. Instead I have tried to present, in as short a text as feasible, a summary of most of the aspects of waterfowl biology that I find of greatest personal interest. This does not mean, however, that I have not relied on the voluminous technical literature dealing with waterfowl; in fact, relatively little of the text represents previously unpublished information. The selected bibliography lists in general recent works that I consider especially pertinent for persons wishing to follow up points of interest found in this book. In short, I have attempted to direct my writing to an audience of nonprofessionals who have little experience with or immediate access to the technical literature, in hopes of providing them with a basic nucleus of biological information and the desire to enlarge on such a foundation through additional reading or personal observations. In thus generalizing my statements and sometimes popularizing my text, I have knowingly run the risk of oversimplification; but I trust that those readers who are professional waterfowl biologists will be charitable if they perceive any exceptions to certain statements.

In the text I have attempted to be as cosmopolitan as possible in my consideration of the waterfowl family, according equal attention to exotic and native waterfowl species. In the background of my work, I am indebted to persons of different nationalities for inspiration and facilitation of my studies. Foremost among these are an American, H. A. Hochbaum; and an Englishman, Peter Scott; and a German, Konrad Lorenz. Al Hochbaum set the pattern for modern field studies on waterfowl biology with his classic *Canvasback on a Prairie Marsh*; he also has influenced the attitudes and shaped the training of a whole generation of waterfowl biologists. Peter Scott transformed an early intense love for waterfowl hunting and painting into an even greater passion for waterfowl conservation and research; he has perhaps done more for the cause of waterfowl appreciation than any other living man. Konrad Lorenz blended an extraordinary sensitivity to the behavior of waterfowl with the keen perception of an evolutionary zoologist, and it was his writings that provided me with a veritable Rosetta stone to the fascinating world of waterfowl ethology. In addition, all these men have assisted me directly in various other ways, for which I am forever grateful. To these three outstanding biologists—and to others like them who share that special indefinable feeling for wild waterfowl that is somehow acquired only by prolonged exposure to marshes, seacoasts, or tundra, and terminated only by death—I dedicate this book.

Finally, I should like to acknowledge the financial assistance of the U. S. Public Health Service and the National Science Foundation for providing post-doctoral fellowships that facilitated most of my earlier waterfowl studies, and to thank the National Science Foundation for supporting my more recent research on the group (N.S.F. grant GB-1030). Acknowledgment is offered for the use of photographs for Plates 28 and 87 (Copyright © 1965 by Cornell University. Used by permission of Cornell University Press). Additionally, photographs for possible inclusion in this book were helpfully provided by Dr. John Beer, Mrs Pamela Harrison, Sven-Axel Bengtson, Thomas Lowe, and Richard Moss. To these and many others who have helped me in countless ways, I offer my sincere thanks.

PAUL A. JOHNSGARD

Lincoln, Nebraska

Contents

List of Illustrations

FIGURES

TABLES

Introduction

WE count ourselves fortunate at Slimbridge to have had Paul Johnsgard working with us for the best part of two years. He certainly set new standards for application and productivity that are the envy of other research workers in the field of animal behavior. A score of specialized papers poured from his typewriter, followed by his massive and definitive *Handbook of Waterfowl Behavior*. This will surely remain a major source text for many years to come.

Now, in the present volume, he has broadened his approach with a presentation that will appeal to a very wide readership; and this is particularly important because the world's waterfowl face an uncertain future and the wider the interest in them, the better the chances of survival. Ducks, geese, and swans are dependent on wetlands, and wetlands are among the most vulnerable habitats where modern technology is concerned. Draining a marsh can so easily be made to appear a constructive act, full of credit to the people who order it. Too often, in reality, the returns are minimal, shattering the intricate balance of the water regime of the area, which may turn the final reckoning into a tragic overall loss. Some wetlands, notably those in and around river mouths, are more biologically productive *as wetlands* than any other kinds of land on earth.

The tempo of drainage in the so-called developing countries is increasing all over the world. Efforts are being made by conservation agencies, such as the International Wildfowl Research Bureau (IWRB), the International Union for Conservation of Nature and Natural Resources (IUCN), the World Wildlife Fund, and our own Wildfowl Trust, to moderate the attack and to preserve outright the most important areas. The help of all concerned persons and organizations is needed to stem the tide of our losses and to advance the cause of conservation throughout the world.

When you have read Paul's masterly, succinct text and reveled in the superb collection of photographs he has assembled, I know you will agree that the world's waterfowl are well worth saving.

PETER SCOTT

The Wildfowl Trust
Slimbridge, England

WATERFOWL

Introduction to
the Waterfowl

*J*UST as waterfowl enthusiasts share many interests in common, so waterfowl themselves have in common many shared characteristics, whether they be ducks, geese, or swans. Such common features are mainly the result of a merging ancestry that extends back at least fifty million years, since definite fossil waterfowl of such an age have been described, and other fossils of possible ancestral waterfowl are much older than this.

Those characteristics shared by all living waterfowl are probably the oldest and most basic in the life of every species. All species of waterfowl thus have feet that are at least partially webbed to increase swimming efficiency, have down-covered young that are able to swim soon after hatching, and have bills of various shapes and differential development of lamellae, which are associated with differing types of feeding behavior.

Within this broad framework of common characteristics, there have evolved individual species that exhibit a remarkable diversity in size, form, behavior, and environmental requirements. Among the living species of waterfowl are birds ranging in size from the diminutive pygmy geese that average ten ounces or so when fully grown, to the Trumpeter Swan that sometimes weighs over thirty pounds and has a wingspread approaching one hundred inches.

Some species are practically omnivorous in their diet. The Ruddy Shelduck, for example, has been observed to eat even the remains of human bodies thrown into the Ganges River of India, whereas others, such as the algae-eating Pink-eared Duck of Australia, have bills highly specialized for utilizing particular food sources and are relatively dependent upon such foods.

A few species occur over immense geographic ranges. The Northern Pintail is found over nearly the entire northern hemisphere; by comparison, the Madagascan White-eye occurs on only a few lakes of that large island. Some of the wider-ranging species such as the Canada Goose vary geographically in size and coloration to such an extent that races and species are very difficult to delineate; however, the Fulvous Whistling Duck is found on four continents in widely separated populations and exhibits no definite geographic variation.

Variations in the general biology and behavior of waterfowl are primarily correlated with their evolutionary relationships within the family Anatidae. It is convenient therefore to discuss within each topic of the following chapters such variations according to the major taxonomic subgroups of classification, which in descending sequence are subfamilies, tribes, genera, species, and subspecies. In the classification used here, which is my own modification of one proposed by Jean Delacour, the family Anatidae is composed of three subfamilies, 11 tribes, 43 genera, and 146 recent species as follows:

Family Anatidae (Ducks, Geese, and Swans)

Subfamily Anseranatinae
    Tribe Anseranatini—Magpie Goose (1 genus and species)
Subfamily Anserinae
    Tribe Dendrocygnini—Whistling or Tree Ducks (2 genera, 9 species)
    Tribe Anserini—Swans and True Geese (5 genera, 21 species)
    Tribe Stictonettini—Freckled Duck (1 genus and species)[1]
Subfamily Anatinae
    Tribe Tadornini—Sheldgeese and Shelducks (5 genera, 15 species)
    Tribe Tachyerini—Steamer Ducks (1 genus, 3 species)[2]
    Tribe Cairinini—Perching Ducks (9 genera, 13 species)
    Tribe Anatini—Dabbling or Surface-feeding Ducks (5 genera, 39 species)
    Tribe Aythyini—Pochards (3 genera, 16 species)
    Tribe Mergini—Sea Ducks (8 genera, 20 species)[3]
    Tribe Oxyurini—Stiff-tailed Ducks (3 genera, 8 species)

These groups are believed to be related to one another in the manner shown by the accompanying diagram, or evolutionary tree. This diagram indicates the

[1] This species is included in the Anatini by Delacour.
[2] This group is included in the Tadornini by Delacour.
[3] Delacour subdivides this group into two tribes.

FIGURE I. Evolutionary tree of the waterfowl family Anatidae. Major branches (tribes) are identified by collective common names; heads illustrate representative species of all forty-three genera of living or recently extinct waterfowl. Broken lines indicate uncertainties of evolutionary relationships.

probable affinities of all the forty-three genera recognized in this book and illustrates the heads of adult males of species representing all these genera (Figure 1). Scientific and preferred English names of all the recent species of Anatidae are to be found in the last chapter of this book; but as an introduction to the entire family, some salient characteristics of the larger groupings (the subfamilies and tribes) will be taken up here.

SUBFAMILY ANSERANATINAE

Tribe Anseranatini (Magpie Goose)

This first subfamily is composed of a single tribe, a single genus, and a single species, the Magpie Goose. This strange black and white gooselike bird ranges through most of Australia and the southern tip of New Guinea, differing from all the rest of the waterfowl in so many respects that it has sometimes been placed in a separate family of its own.

Foremost among the Magpie Goose's obvious peculiarities are its feet that are webbed only slightly and its long hind toes that are related to the bird's semiterrestrial adaptations and its frequent perching. Like the rest of the waterfowl family, this species molts its wing feathers once a year; but in contrast to nearly all other waterfowl, molting of the flight feathers is done gradually so that the bird retains its ability to fly. In this respect, as in the case of many of their anatomical features, Magpie Geese resemble the South American wading birds called screamers (family Anhimidae), which together with the Anatidae comprise the order Anseriformes. It thus appears that Magpie Geese may provide an evolutionary link between the true waterfowl and other bird groups. If this is the case, the Magpie Goose can probably be looked upon as the most generalized waterfowl species; that is, it possesses the greatest number of primitive features of all living waterfowl. Indeed, if a person were to try to reconstruct an ancestral species that gave rise to all the presently existing forms of waterfowl, it would seem that the Magpie Goose might provide a number of clues. A few very ancient waterfowl fossils dating back to the Eocene period have been described, but these are only tiny fragments and give little knowledge of what the first waterfowl species must have been like (Figure 2). Some biologists think that waterfowl developed from a gallinaceous ancestor distantly related to the family of birds now represented by such species as the chachalacas, while others believe that the more aquatic flamingos and storklike birds are their nearest living relatives. Anatomical similarities among the Magpie Goose, the screamers, and the chachalaca family tend to favor the first theory.

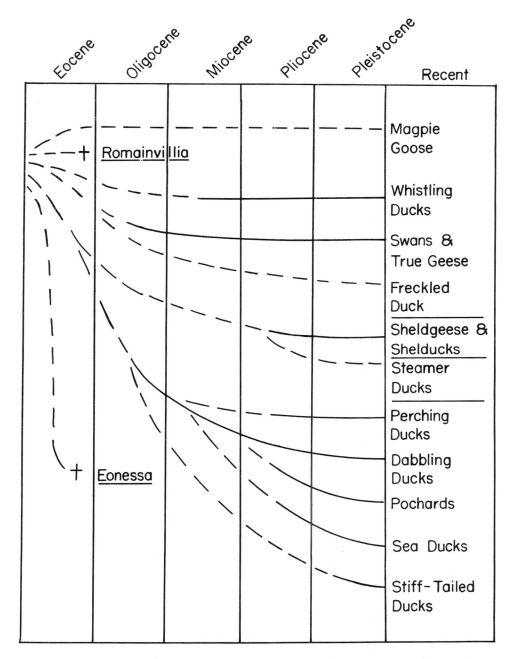

FIGURE 2. Fossil history of the waterfowl family Anatidae. Unbroken lines indicate relatively continuous fossil records for each tribe into past geologic periods (epochs). Broken lines indicate absence of fossil record for indicated periods. The relationships of the two Eocene genera shown are questionable. This diagram is based on information presented by Howard (in Delacour, 1964).

SUBFAMILY ANSERINAE

The subfamily Anserinae includes the whistling ducks, the swans, and the true geese. Although all the species are related only distantly to the Magpie Goose, they share with it several features. They undergo only a single molt each year, which occurs after the breeding season and during which all feathers are replaced. Unlike the Magpie Goose, flight feathers are shed almost simultaneously, so that the birds are unable to fly for a period of about three to six weeks. In common with the Magpie Goose, the unfeathered tarsus or lower leg has an irregular network or reticulated surface pattern throughout, but the toes are more fully webbed. In all species, the sexes are essentially identical in plumage, differing primarily in body size and, occasionally, in voice. None of the species perch to the same degree as does the Magpie Goose, not even the "tree ducks," as the whistling ducks are commonly called. In addition, all species totally lack iridescent coloration. Although most authorities consider the Freckled Duck of Australia to be a member of the subfamily Anatinae, it exhibits the above-mentioned features and is here considered to comprise a special tribe in this subfamily.

Tribe Dendrocygnini (Whistling Ducks)

The whistling ducks are a group of nine species, eight of which are placed in the single genus *Dendrocygna*, or "tree swans." Although rather swanlike or gooselike in behavior, they are not primarily perching birds, and thus "tree ducks" is an equally misleading name. A far better name is whistling ducks, for in all species the voice of both sexes is a clear, usually multisyllabic whistle. Most of the species are tropical or semitropical in distribution, and evidently little if any migration occurs in the more tropical species. These birds range in size from less than one pound in the Lesser Whistling Duck to more than two pounds in the Black-billed Whistling Duck. They differ from geese, and from all other waterfowl as well, in the pattern of their downy young. The ducklings tend to be strongly marked, with a characteristic light stripe that extends under the eyes and back around the nape without interruption. Adult plumages vary considerably, but the broad rounded wings, long legs and necks, and large feet combine to produce a distinctive appearance. Recently obtained behavioral and anatomical evidence strongly favors the inclusion of the African and Madagascan White-backed Duck in this group, rather than considering it as an aberrant stiff-tailed duck. Adult White-backed Ducks have whistling voices, perform incubation and brood care by both sexes, and have mating behavior patterns that are shared in common with the typical whistling ducks.

Tribe Anserini (Swans and True Geese)

The swans and true geese are moderately large to extremely large waterfowl, which in common with the whistling ducks have plumage patterns that are alike in both sexes, lack iridescent coloration, and have reticulated tarsal surfaces. Most of the twenty-one species are found in the northern hemisphere, the exceptions being three species of swans and one unusual Australian goose, the Cape Barren Goose. This latter species is sometimes regarded as constituting a separate tribe or is included with the sheldgeese, and its downy young are very much like those of the sheldgeese. The more typical geese and swans have downy young that lack complex patterning. Adult plumages are likewise generally similar, without strong pattern contrasts, although a few species have strikingly beautiful adult plumages. Almost all the species have considerable amounts of white in the plumage, but in some of the geese this is restricted to the undertail coverts. Swans and geese normally require two or three years to attain reproductive maturity, whereas most ducks mature in their first year.

Tribe Stictonettini (Freckled Duck)

On the basis of its somewhat gooselike skeletal anatomy, its possession of a reticulated tarsal surface, its gray, unpatterned downy young, and its lack of an elaborate adult plumage pattern or complex vocal apparatus, the Freckled Duck of Australia deserves inclusion in the subfamily Anserinae. What has so far been learned about the species' reproductive behavior also suggests anserine affinities, but unfortunately very little information is presently available regarding this aspect of its biology.

SUBFAMILY ANATINAE

This last and largest subfamily, Anatinae, includes the sheldgeese, shelducks, and all the typical ducks. It is divided into numerous tribes, of which seven are recognized here. In most if not all the species included in this subfamily, there are two molts of the body feathers and consequently there are usually two distinct plumages, breeding ("nuptial") and nonbreeding (winter or "eclipse"). In some species the breeding plumage of the male resembles that of the female, but more often the sexes have very different breeding plumages. Likewise, the voices of the sexes are normally very different in species of this subfamily. This vocal difference is evidently the result of an asymmetrical bony enlargement, termed a "bulla," in the male's syrinx, the vocal organ of the trachea (see Figure 5). Another basic anatomical difference is that the front surface of the lower tarsus has linearly arranged (scutellated) scales, as opposed to the network pattern or reticulated surface typical of all the preceding groups. Downy plumages in the various tribes tend to be distinctly patterned, usually with spots and stripes on the head and back. Adult plumages are generally rather elaborate, and iridescent coloration is frequent, especially on males. Iridescent coloration on females is usually restricted to the region of the secondary wing feathers; such conspicuous wing patterns are called speculums. Where the sexes differ in plumage, the male is typically more brightly colored and more elaborately patterned, though there are a few interesting exceptions. In addition, the plumage of juveniles and the adult male's nonbreeding plumage generally resemble that of the female. Finally, males of many species (and females of a few) have finely barred, or vermiculated, feather patterns on the back and flanks.

Tribe Tadornini (Sheldgeese and Shelducks)

The most gooselike species of this subfamily are the sheldgeese, which together with the closely related shelducks comprise the tribe Tadornini. This group of fifteen species has a worldwide distribution except for North America. It is difficult to make a clear distinction between the true geese and the sheldgeese, for the Cape Barren Goose partly bridges the gap between them and might be logically placed in either group. The species here included in the tribe, however, all exhibit enlarged tracheal bullas (in the males) and have corresponding major differences in the voices of the sexes. Many species also have widely differing adult plumages in the two sexes, although a few have almost no sexual differences in appearance. With few exceptions, the species in this tribe have white upper and under wing coverts, and iridescent green wing speculums. The downy plumages of nearly all species are strongly patterned with black and white. Iridescent coloration occurs primarily on the speculum, and in the Egyptian Goose and the shelducks this speculum pattern is formed by the secondary feathers, which is usually the case among ducks. In the typical sheldgeese, however, it is formed by the secondary coverts, and the secondaries themselves form a broad white posterior border.

Tribe Tachyerini (Steamer Ducks)

The South American steamer ducks are sometimes included with the shelducks, though they differ enough from shelducks that they are now often regarded as a separate tribe. There are apparently three species, all closely related and placed in a single genus. They are very large ducks, and two of the species are essentially flightless. They all are found off the coast of southern South America and the Falkland Islands, where they feed on mollusks and other marine animal life. The males differ somewhat from females in both plumage and voice, but both sexes lack bright coloration and have only a simple white wing patch. The downy young resemble to some extent those of shelducks, but have little spotting and less contrasting coloration.

Tribe Cairinini (Perching Ducks)

This group of thirteen species of primarily perching waterfowl is a rather heterogeneous assemblage that is not easily characterized. In addition to being perching birds and sometimes also semiterrestrial, they generally have wide, rounded wings, elongated tails and, in some species, relatively long legs. Many species have a great deal of iridescent coloration in their plumage, while in a few species almost all the body feathers of both sexes are colored in this manner. There is a remarkable difference in the sizes of the sexes in some species, such as the Comb Duck. In this species the adult male is practically twice as heavy as the female. Iridescent wing plumage is typical in this tribe, and some remarkably elaborate speculum patterns are to be found in its members as well. In spite of the generally marked sexual differences, males of only a few species exhibit definite eclipse plumages. This may be related to the fact that many are tropical birds and their breeding seasons are often long or irregular. In the patterns of their downy young, the perching ducks are very similar to the dabbling ducks; both groups have ducklings that are contrastingly colored with yellow or white and darker tones, typically with distinct back spotting and eye-stripes. Most perching ducks are cavity nesters, and both the adults and downy young have sharply clawed toes that facilitate perching and climbing.

Tribe Anatini (Dabbling Ducks)

The dabbling or surface-feeding ducks are, judging from the number and abundance of the species, the most successful of all waterfowl. This group includes all the "puddle ducks" which constitute most of the important game species. Of the thirty-nine species comprising the tribe, all but four can be readily placed in the single genus *Anas*. The tribe has a worldwide distribution, many of the species being found on several continents. On the whole, however, the dabbling ducks mostly breed in temperate climates, and many of them migrate considerable distances during the nonbreeding period. In most dabblers the males have fairly elaborate plumage patterns, whereas the ground-nesting females are mostly cryptic-colored, with buff and brown markings. Nearly all species have iridescent wing speculums, and males of all dabblers have enlarged bony tracheal bullas. The plumages of the downy young are conspicuously patterned, usually dark brown with buffy or yellow markings on the back and head. In three of the four aberrant species often included in the tribe, the bill structure is highly modified to provide unusual feeding adaptations. One of these species, the Andean Torrent Duck, is a highly specialized stream-dwelling form sometimes placed in a tribe of its own (Merganettini).

Tribe Aythyini (Pochards)

This tribe of fresh-water diving ducks contains sixteen species that are collectively called pochards. The tribe has a worldwide distribution, but only a few pochards have ranges extending over more than one continent. Besides fifteen species of typical pochards, the apparently extinct Pink-headed Duck shares certain anatomical features with these birds and clearly should be included in the tribe. All the typical pochards are adept at diving and possess large feet and strongly lobed hind toes. Their legs are also relatively widely spread, short, and placed farther back on the body than in the dabbling ducks, making pochards relatively awkward on land but increasing their diving efficiency. Iridescent coloration is lacking on the wings and is restricted to the heads of a few species. Although sexual dimorphism occurs to some extent in all species, male plumage patterns are not especially elaborate or complex. Wing speculums are lacking or are limited to gray or white stripes. The plumage patterns of pochard ducklings are generally similar to those found in the preceding tribe except that distinct eye-stripes and cheek-stripes are usually lacking. The female's plumage is characteristically rather uniformly brownish and lacks the distinctly disruptive patterning typical of female dabbling ducks.

Tribe Mergini (Sea Ducks)

The sea duck tribe, which here includes the eiders, consists of twenty species that are all superb diving birds. They are found in both fresh water and marine environments and are primarily of northern hemisphere distribution. Except for the two isolated southern hemisphere species, all sea ducks have considerable sexual dimorphism in plumage. The male's nuptial plumage is usually elaborately patterned, often with black and white contrasts predominating. Iridescent coloration occurs in the wing speculums of two species, but is otherwise restricted to the heads of males. Many of the sea ducks do have large white speculum patterns, although a few species lack wing pattern specializations completely. Females of the larger ground-nesting eiders have disruptively colored brownish bodies strikingly similar to those of dabbling ducks, but females of the other ground- or cavity-nesting species are more uniformly grayish or brownish. Downy plumages are quite variable and range from the eiders' brownish and rather obscurely patterned ducklings, through the black and white bicolored patterns of the scoters and goldeneyes, to the contrastingly spotted or streaked brown and white patterns of the mergansers.

Tribe Oxyurini (Stiff-tailed Ducks)

The stiff-tailed ducks are characterized by several unusual features in addition to their long, stiffened tail feathers that serve as underwater rudders. Among other adaptations for diving are the very large feet, which are placed so far back on the body that it is difficult for these species to walk on land. The body feathers are small, shiny, and numerous, giving the birds a grebelike aspect, and the wings are so short that they make flight appear difficult. All the species have short, thick necks which in males can be enlarged by the inflation of various internal structures. Although most species exhibit sexual dimorphism in plumage, the male plumages are not elaborate nor is iridescent coloration present in any. The downy patterns are generally inconspicuous and typically resemble the adult female's plumage. Nonbreeding male plumages similar to those of the female occur in most of the eight species here included in the tribe. Except for two aberrant species, the male breeding plumages are quite similar and include heads that are partially or entirely black, bodies of ruddy coloration, and bluish bills. The two species that do not fit this general description are the Musk Duck of Australia and the South American Black-headed Duck. The Musk Duck may be considered a very large and somewhat grotesque relative of the true "ruddy ducks," but the Black-headed Duck appears to be a definite evolutionary link between these more typical stiff-tails and the dabbling ducks. The White-backed Duck, usually considered to be a member of this tribe, has only remote similarities to the stiff-tails and in this book is included with the whistling ducks.

↑ 1. Plumed Whistling Duck (pair)   ↓ 2. Fulvous Whistling Duck (family)

3. Wandering Whistling Duck

4. Black-billed Whistling Duck

5. Mute Swan (general shake)

↑ 6. Mute Swan (preening)   ↓ 7. Black Swan (pair)

8. Whooper Swan (female and young)

9. Bewick's Swan (foreground) and Whistling Swan

↑ 10. Trumpeter Swan (adult male)   ↓ 11. Swan Goose

↑ 12. Pink-footed Goose (pair)   ↓ 13. Graylag Goose (threat display)

14. White-fronted Goose (pair)

↑ 15. Bar-headed Goose (molting)　　　　　　　↓ 16. Snow Goose

17. "Blue" phase of Snow Goose (male calling)

↑ 18. Ross' Goose (pair)   ↓ 19. Giant Canada Goose (male)

↑ 20. Barnacle Goose (pair)   ↓ 21. Black Brant Goose (female)

↑ 22. Andean Goose (female)

↓ 23. Kelp Goose (pair)

↑ 24. Ashy-headed Goose (male)   ↓ 25. Ruddy-headed Goose (family)

Distribution
and Migrations

WATERFOWL occur on every continent except
Antarctica and on every major island of the world. Most of the species are primarily fresh-water birds, but some species of geese, steamer ducks, and sea ducks maintain a rather distinctly maritime existence, feeding to a large degree on such ocean foods as kelp and mussels.

Relatively few waterfowl species inhabit both the northern and southern hemispheres; in fact, the Fulvous Whistling Duck is the only waterfowl species that breeds in all hemispheres, from North America to India. Apart from this bird, the only waterfowl which breed in both North and South America are the Ruddy Duck and the Cinnamon Teal. Both these species, unlike the Fulvous Whistling Duck, vary markedly in size and male plumage coloration in different parts of their ranges. In South America they are evidently less migratory than in North America; the populations that inhabit the lakes of the Andean ranges are probably completely sedentary. North American populations of both these species, however, are strongly migratory, and at least the Cinnamon Teal may winter as far south as northern South America. Like the Fulvous Whistling Duck, the Red-billed Whistling Duck practically qualifies as a Pan-American species too, although its breeding range scarcely reaches the southernmost part of the United States.

In the old world, the only species that distinctly qualifies as a breeding bird through much of both northern and southern hemispheres is an Australasian equivalent of the Mallard that is called the Spot-billed Duck in India, Burma, and China, and the "Gray Duck" or "Black Duck" in New Zealand and Australia. Many authorities consider these populations to comprise two species, but it is in keeping with modern classification to consider such geographic variations as subspecies. One other species, the Cotton Pygmy Goose, is found in both hemispheres from southern China to northern Australia, but does not exhibit such a distinctly bihemispheric distribution as the others that have been mentioned. It is curious that all these examples are ducks, and that no geese or swans should have been able to colonize both the northern and southern hemispheres. Perhaps this is because the geese and swans tend to be temperate- and arctic-breeding birds that may not be so able to spread successfully across tropical regions. However, the Canada Goose has been successfully introduced into New Zealand.

It is much more common for a species to occupy both the eastern and western hemispheres, a situation especially true of north temperate and arctic species. Of the swans, the Trumpeter-Whooper and Whistling-Bewick's groups have extensive ranges in both the eastern and western hemispheres. The White-fronted Goose has a broad circumpolar breeding range which is perhaps the most extensive of any of the geese. The Brant Goose is a maritime species that occurs over most of the high arctic seacoasts. It is strange that none of the shelducks occur in both the eastern and western hemispheres. Their complete absence from North America makes one wonder if there is not an available ecological habitat there that remains to be occupied some day by a shelduck colonization. None of the perching ducks have transhemispheric ranges in the northern hemisphere, 'but the more migratory dabbling ducks have obviously not regarded the oceans as a major barrier. No less than five species, including the Common Mallard, Northern Green-winged Teal, Gadwall, Northern Pintail, and Northern Shoveler occur throughout most of the north temperate zone, and only in the case of the teal does the North American population differ markedly from the old world form. The pochards are evidently more provincial than the dabblers, for only the Greater Scaup is a cosmopolite, occurring widely in both hemispheres. The oceans present no barriers to the sea ducks, however, and two of the three species of scoters, all four eiders, the Harlequin Duck, the Long-tailed Duck or Oldsquaw, both species of goldeneyes, and two species of mergansers have ranges extending well into both hemispheres.

Transhemispheric distributions in the southern hemisphere are much less frequent, probably as a result of the greater ocean distances generally encountered. South America shares only four species with Africa (White-faced Whistling Duck,

Fulvous Whistling Duck, Comb Duck, and Southern Pochard), and none with Australia. Africa likewise shares no waterfowl species with Australia.

It has already been mentioned that the Fulvous Whistling Duck has perhaps the broadest overall distribution of any waterfowl species including parts of North and South America; Africa, Madagascar, and India. However, in terms of relative abundance it is likely that species such as the Common Mallard and Northern Pintail edge out the Fulvous Whistling Duck; these two species occur in incalculable numbers throughout the extensive waterfowl habitat of the northern tundra and prairies of Europe, Asia, and North America.

It is also interesting to consider some of the cases of very restricted distributions among waterfowl. Considering full species only, the swans, geese, and whistling ducks all tend to have extensive ranges. Only the Hawaiian Goose, or Nene, which probably was derived from a continental form ancestral to the Canada Goose, has a small, island distribution, and the Black-billed and Spotted Whistling Ducks are limited to the West Indies and East Indies respectively. The shelducks and sheldgeese are sometimes relatively restricted in distribution. The Kelp Goose, for example, is found only along the southern tip of Chile and the Falkland Islands, and is probably geographically limited to the range of the kelp on which it feeds. The Blue-winged Goose is found only in the Ethiopian highlands of north-eastern Africa above 8,000 feet, and the Cape Shelduck is indigenous only to South Africa. Steamer ducks occur in much the same regions as the Kelp Goose, and they too are probably restricted by their diet to these temperate coastal areas.

Among the dabbling ducks, pochards, and perching ducks, broad continental distributions seem to be the rule. But in Madagascar three rare ducks are found: the Meller's Duck, the Madagascan White-eye, and the Madagascan Teal (Figure 3). All these birds have a very restricted distribution but are evidently very close relatives of three more wide-ranging species (Mallard, Ferruginous White-eye, and Gray Teal). The little-studied Brown Teal of New Zealand may likewise be an island derivative of the Chestnut Teal, but it has been suggested that the bird might be a descendant of a relatively primitive and presumably once more wide-ranging species. The Philippine Duck is almost certainly an island form of the Mallard and "Spot-bill" group but is apparently a distinct species that has become markedly modified from the original stock. Both the Blue Duck of the New Zealand torrential streams, and the Salvadori's Duck, which occupies the mountain lakes and streams of New Guinea, are examples of species having restricted distributions probably related to habitat or feeding specializations. The Torrent Duck of South America is an example of a bird that is geographically very widespread but ecologically highly limited in occurrence to mountain torrents

FIGURE 3. Examples of waterfowl species having highly restricted ranges. The birds illustrated are all males. Upper left: Madagascan White-eye. Upper right: Meller's Duck of Madagascar. Middle left: Kerguelen Island race of Pintail. Middle right: South Georgia Island race of Yellow-billed Pintail. Lower left: Madagascan Teal. Lower right: Laysan Island race of Mallard ("Laysan Teal").

of the Andes. The Baer's Pochard occurs in parts of eastern Asia, but the exact range of that apparently rare species is still uncertain.

There are several cases of restricted distributions in the sea ducks. The rarely seen Spectacled Eider is limited to the coasts of Alaska and northeastern Siberia, and the smaller Steller's Eider has a similar breeding range. Both are reputed to winter mainly in the Aleutian Islands, although there have never been discovered any wintering concentrations of the Spectacled Eider. The now extinct Labrador Duck had a breeding range that might have centered around Labrador. The Auckland Island Merganser, also now almost certainly extinct, had what is probably the most restricted distribution of any full species of waterfowl, being found only on the tiny Auckland Islands, about four hundred miles south of New Zealand, with no other merganser species occurring for several thousand miles.

Island races of continental species are common in waterfowl, especially among the wide-ranging dabbling ducks. There are small, inbred races of the Mallard on both the Hawaiian Islands and Laysan Island (Figure 3). There are similar island races of the Pintail on the subantarctic islands of Kerguelen and Crozet, thousands of miles south of the Northern Pintail's normal range (Figure 3). Likewise, the now extinct Coues' race of Gadwall was found on the remote Fanning Islands about one thousand miles south of Hawaii. Other less dramatic cases are the Galapagos Islands race of the Bahama Pintail, the South Georgia Island race of the Yellow-billed Pintail (Figure 3), and the Auckland and Campbell Islands races of the Brown Teal of New Zealand. All these island races share the disadvantages of being relatively small, greatly inbred populations in danger of extinction if conditions should become unfavorable for them.

PATTERNS OF DISTRIBUTION

If we tally the ranges of the species of waterfowl according to the generally accepted zoogeographic regions of the world, some interesting patterns can be seen (Table 1). For example, no tribe of waterfowl is uniformly distributed around the world, although the nearly ubiquitous dabbling ducks approach this condition. Although a few of the less specialized waterfowl groups (whistling ducks, perching ducks) clearly have their headquarters in the tropics or the southern hemisphere, it is evident that the northern hemisphere typically supports a larger variety of species, notably the swans, geese, pochards, and sea ducks. It would appear that the waterfowl may have had their early origins in tropical or southern regions, but that they have been more successful in the extensive grasslands and tundras of the north temperate and arctic zones.

TABLE 1

Distribution of Indigenous Breeding Waterfowl Species by Zoogeographic Regions

	Pale-arctic[1]	Nearc-tic[2]	Neo-tropical[3]	Austra-lian[4]	Ethio-pian[5]	Orien-tal[6]
Magpie Goose (1 sp.)	—	—	—	1	—	—
Whistling Ducks (9 spp.)	—	2	4	2	3	3
Swans and Geese (21 spp.)	15	9	2	2	—	—
Freckled Duck (1 sp.)	—	—	—	1	—	—
Sheldgeese and Shelducks (15 spp.)	4	—	6	2	3	—
Steamer Ducks (3 spp.)	—	—	3	—	—	—
Perching Ducks (13 spp.)	2	1	4	3	4	3
Dabbling Ducks (39 spp.)	11	9	10	8	8	3
Pochards (16 spp.)	6	5	2	2	2	1
Sea Ducks (20 spp.)	14	16	1	1	—	—
Stiff-tailed Ducks (8 spp.)	1	1	3	2	1	—
Totals	53	43	35	24	21	10

[1] Europe, Asia north of the Himalayas, and northern Africa
[2] North America, Greenland, northern Mexico, and Hawaiian Islands
[3] South and Central America (except Mexican uplands), and West Indies
[4] Australia, New Zealand, New Guinea, Melanesia, and Polynesia
[5] Africa (except northern part), southern Arabia, and Madagascar
[6] India, Southeast Asia, Sumatra, Java, Borneo, and Philippine Islands

MIGRATIONS

Because the great waterfowl breeding grounds of North America, Europe, and Asia all have temperate to arctic climates and are unsuitable as wintering areas for water birds, migration in waterfowl is primarily a northern hemisphere phenomenon, or at least is most conspicuous here. In the southern hemisphere climatic extremes occur only in southern South America, and the area affected there by cold winters is much smaller.

In North America, waterfowl migrations tend to follow the north-south "flyway" patterns that have been described in many books, although it is clear that these "aerial highways" are not nearly so rigidly adhered to by birds as once believed.

American waterfowl having the longest migration routes are probably the Cinnamon Teal and Blue-winged Teal, two of our smallest species. The Blue-winged Teal breeds as far north as the Canadian sub-arctic (60° north latitude), but also occasionally nests as far south as Florida. Sometimes it winters south of the equator; the most southerly specimen record is for a bird shot recently in Chile's Coquino Province (31° 54′ south latitude), but the species has also been seen near Buenos Aires, Argentina. One Blue-winged Teal that had been banded in Saskatchewan was recovered six months later in Peru, over seven thousand miles from the point of banding, and another, banded in Alberta, was recovered a month later nearly four thousand miles away in Venezuela.

In Europe and Asia, migration distances are probably somewhat longer on the average than in North America, and the routes often deviate considerably from a strict north-south direction. The Northern Shoveler, Northern Pintail, and European Wigeon all breed beyond the Arctic Circle to at least 70° north latitude, and they may winter as far south as central Africa to the equator. There are even some possible records for the Northern Shoveler in South Africa. The Northern Green-winged Teal and Garganey have only slightly less extensive migratory routes than these species.

In South America it is probable that only such species as some sheldgeese, the Silver Teal, Bronze-winged Duck, South American Green-winged Teal, and a few others inhabiting the southern tip of South America are markedly migratory. It is also evident that various ducks which breed in the interior marshes of Argentina move out of these areas during the dry winter season. Some vertical migration definitely occurs in the Andean Torrent Duck. Unfortunately, however, almost nothing is yet definitely known concerning migrations and wintering areas of South American ducks.

In Africa and particularly in Australia, seasonal movements are probably more dependent upon water conditions than upon seasonal fluctuations in temperature. This is especially evident in Australia where, in some years, many thousands of waterfowl will breed in temporary water areas, only to disappear afterward and not return until conditions once again become favorable.

It seems possible that the world record for migratory flight distance among the waterfowl would fall to the Blue-winged Teal, some members of which may migrate as much as seven thousand miles from northern Canada to central South America, or to the Northern Shoveler, which could have a similar maximum migratory distance from northern Europe to south-central Africa. It is obvious, however, that the great majority of birds of even these species migrate considerably shorter distances, and it also may be stated that in many cases individual members of a species tend to fly only the minimum distance necessary to attain a habitat suitable for spending the nonbreeding period. Because male ducks are usually somewhat larger than females, they can tolerate slightly colder temperatures; and so in the colder parts of the wintering ranges males usually predominate, while in the warmer parts of the wintering range females are often more abundant.

The means by which waterfowl find their way on migration is a complex topic that will not be taken up here, since an authoritative book by H. A. Hochbaum thoroughly discusses this fascinating problem. Recent work by such people as Frank Bellrose, William Hamilton, and Geoffrey Matthews has clearly proven the importance of both the sun and the stars as orientation aids. For example, William Hamilton was able to train young hand-reared Blue-winged Teal to orient correctly in a testing apparatus by using either the sun or stars as clues, but the birds' orientation failed when neither of these was directly visible. Such sensory abilities would appear to provide the navigational basis for long-range migrations, as well as for initial orientation in unfamiliar environments.

Geoffrey Matthews has released hundreds of wild Common Mallards in various areas away from their place of capture, finding that such displaced birds exhibit an initial "nonsense orientation," so-called because if either the sun or the stars are visible, a constant initial directional orientation is taken, regardless of the proper "home" direction. This orientation ability is maintained in different seasons, but by shifting the ducks' "internal clocks" by prolonged exposure to experimentally altered light-dark cycles, Dr. Matthews found that such birds modify such sun-orientation by an angle corresponding to the amount of their time-shifting. However, their star-orientation tendencies were not affected by this treatment. The moon appears to be of little if any value to ducks for their nocturnal orientation, instead it seems possible that constellation patterns are recognized and may be used in a manner similar to that of humans when determining directions at night.

It appears probable that such orientation and navigational abilities of waterfowl are innate and thus need not be learned, but undoubtedly many individually acquired responses do influence the selecting of migration stopover points as well as the use of specific wintering and breeding grounds. By destroying such learned "traditions" through local drainage, over-hunting, or similar activities, a productive area can be rendered permanently useless for waterfowl utilization, and our environment thus becomes that much the poorer.

Ecology and
General Behavior

*I*T might be assumed that the only habitat which the waterfowl group could not possibly utilize would be one totally lacking water. Though most unusual, several species have in fact become adapted to a highly terrestrial existence. The Magpie Goose, for example, is a relatively terrestrial bird, with greatly reduced foot webbing, that is nonetheless able to swim rather well. It is clear that the Hawaiian Goose has become highly adapted to a mountainous environment where standing water is practically absent. Even in captivity this goose swims only infrequently, and its webbing is distinctly reduced. Furthermore, mating occurs on land, and so the need for having water nearby to insure successful fertilization is absent. The same evidently applies to at least one other species, the Cape Barren Goose; it too has a reduced foot webbing and has similarly become adapted to a semiterrestrial existence.

The saltwater environment has been colonized by two diverse groups of waterfowl, the sea ducks of the northern hemisphere and the shelducks and steamer ducks of the southern hemisphere. The similarity in feeding habits and appearance exhibited by the South American steamer ducks and the northern hemisphere eiders provides one of the best examples of evolutionary convergence exhibited by waterfowl. In such marine-dwelling ducks physiological adaptations allowing for the drinking of sea water have been developed; and in these, as in other sea birds, the supraorbital glands have been enlarged to provide a means of excreting salts which pass out in solution through the nostrils.

Freshwater ponds and potholes are the favorite breeding habitat for the dabbling ducks, pochards, stiff-tails, and whistling ducks. The perching ducks generally prefer wooded rivers or ponds, where nesting cavities are readily available, and the shelducks usually select similar areas or places where there are crevices or holes that provide nesting sites. Some of the sea ducks, such as the goldeneyes and some mergansers, also normally nest in cavities, but others, such as the eiders and scoters, typically nest on the open tundra or prairie.

Mountainous streams provide suitable breeding habitats for only the most specialized and adaptable species, but several groups of waterfowl have representative ducks that make such streams their home. These are the Torrent Duck of South America, the Salvadori's Duck of New Guinea, the Blue Duck of New Zealand, and the Harlequin Duck of the northern hemisphere.

In feeding adaptations, the waterfowl are equally diversified. The closest approach to an omnivorous diet is perhaps that of the Magpie Goose, which, with its massive and sharp-pointed bill, is able to graze, browse, or root out practically every form of vegetable material.

Swans might be termed aquatic grazers, for they are particularly well adapted for harvesting the rich source of aquatic plant food of the temperate and arctic ponds and streams. Geese are, to a greater extent, terrestrial grazers. The grasses and sedges of the prairies and tundra are optimum food sources of these herbivores, which have bills beautifully adapted to clipping such vegetation (Plates 11 and 16).

In South America similar grazing-type bills have been independently developed by some of the sheldgeese. The so-called Maned Goose and Spur-winged Goose are, in reality, perching ducks, having evolved gooselike bills that allow them to exploit similar foraging opportunities in Australia and Africa respectively. The sharp-pointed lamellae lining the sturdy bills of such gooselike birds provide serrated edges for cutting through grass and other vegetation. The elaboration of these lamellae into a complex comblike structure has provided the waterfowl with a fundamentally different means of feeding too. By taking a mixture of water and edible material into the mouth, squirting the water out the sides of the bill, and retaining the solid edible materials, they have developed an efficient means of gathering small aquatic food. This method of feeding, which is also utilized by flamingos, is an important foraging adaptation in most ducks. Species feeding in this way tend to have flattened, broad bills, a reduced nail, and long lamellae. The Coscoroba Swan has a bill of this type (Plate 35), as do the whistling ducks, some shelducks, and most true ducks. This method of foraging reaches its ultimate degree of refinement in the shovelers and, particularly, in the Pink-eared Duck. The lamellae of this Australian species are so long and closely spaced, and the bill structure so highly modified, that minute algae are readily filtered from the water and provide an important food source.

Animal material is a primary food constituent of several groups of waterfowl. Torrent Ducks, in this category, have long, tapered bills adapted for probing in stream bottoms under rocks for aquatic insect larvae and snails. The Blue Duck forages in a similar manner, and also probably consumes a mixture of animal and vegetable material scraped off wet rocks with its unusually soft-edged and flattened bill. The scaups, more than the other pochards, tend to consume primarily invertebrate animals. Mollusks and shellfish are favorite foods of the larger eiders, scoters, and steamer ducks, whose strong bills are capable of crushing hard-shelled invertebrates. The Steller's Eider and extinct Labrador Duck have bills that are relatively soft at the edges and seem to be adapted for handling more soft-shelled invertebrates, though little is known of the natural foods of these species. In the mergansers one can observe a transition in bill shape from the rather generalized bill of the Smew that resembles those of the goldeneyes, to the remarkably specialized bills of the larger mergansers, which are perfectly designed fish-catching devices. In typical mergansers the bill lamellae are sharply pointed and directed backward, and the nail is in effect a hook, assuring that the slightest hold obtained on a fish or other prey will not be lost (Plate 144). One other species of duck, the Musk Duck of Australia, has also become adapted to a carnivorous diet. The bill of this species is large and massive, without structural specialization, and apparently the Musk Duck's diet is a rather generalized assortment of vertebrates and invertebrates.

GENERAL BEHAVIOR

All waterfowl are accomplished swimmers. It is likely that all waterfowl can also dive if necessary in order to escape capture, but diving is normally used as a foraging technique by only certain groups of waterfowl. The whistling ducks are good divers, in spite of their long legs and anteriorly placed feet, and they are not forced to open their wings when submerging. Shelducks and perching ducks only rarely dive for food, but when doing so they invariably open their wings to assist themselves in submerging. Even the steamer ducks, known to be frequent divers, customarily open their wings when diving. The dabbling ducks dive for food to a greater extent than is generally appreciated, although this occurs more frequently in some species than in others. Most dabblers open their wings while diving, but some smaller species such as the Cape Teal evidently never do so. The stream-dwelling Blue Duck opens its wings, though surprisingly enough it does not appear to be a particularly efficient diving bird, at least as compared to Torrent

Ducks. All the pochards dive admirably without opening their wings and normally forage in this manner. They will, however, tip-up or upend themselves in shallow water, as will most other ducks.

All species of sea ducks dive readily. The larger eiders, being more bulky in body size than most other species, typically open their wings when diving, although I have seen young birds diving without doing so. Because the Steller's Eider and Long-tailed Duck are less heavy, however, they open their wings only slightly or not at all when diving. The latter species has been known to reach depths in excess of 150 feet. Black Scoters often dive without opening their wings, but the larger White-winged Scoter typically uses them. When progressing under water, birds of this species hold their wings slightly open and appear to use them as steering devices. The Surf Scoter may also use its wings for propulsion purposes. The goldeneyes and mergansers normally hold their wings tightly against their bodies while diving and when under water, keeping their flight feathers dry, an obvious advantage if they should have to take flight suddenly.

Stiff-tailed ducks are consummate divers, gliding under the surface without the least apparent effort and frequently remaining under water from fifteen to thirty seconds while foraging. The Black-headed Duck, however, dives more poorly than the typical stiff-tails, and this may help to explain why it usually feeds by tipping-up.

The aquatic foraging of waterfowl which falls outside the pattern of diving for food usually consists of upending (or tipping-up) and surface-feeding. Many swans, geese, and some ducks perform vertical foot-paddling movements when feeding in water that is deeper than can be obtained by reaching down while tipping-up. This foot movement agitates the water and brings food particles nearer the surface, where they can be easily extracted. Northern and Radjah Shelducks often walk about in shallow water, making sidewise sweeping movements of the bill as they dabble for food among the rocks or in the mud. Shovelers, and to a smaller extent most other surface-feeding ducks, have perfected the gathering of floating food by swimming about in the water with the bill at the water surface, dabbling continuously and so gathering food from a broad area. These birds often follow in the wake of other ducks of their own or other species, thus gathering both the usual floating food and also submerged materials that are drawn to the surface in the wake of the preceding bird. Such social feeding often takes the form of a circle when the leading bird begins to follow one of the trailing members.

As flying animals, the waterfowl have few peers among the nonsoaring birds. The heaviest of all flying birds are probably the Trumpeter and Mute Swans, and the power manifested by a flock of flying swans must be seen and heard to be fully appreciated. During sustained flight, swans and Magpie Geese beat their wings about three to four times per second, and most ducks average between six and eight beats per second. It is generally held that the fastest flying waterfowl is the Canvasback whose flight speed has been estimated in excess of 70 miles per hour. When taking flight from land or water, all the swans require a considerable running start against the wind. Geese also normally make such a start as well; however, some smaller geese such as Pink-feet are capable of launching themselves directly into the air from a resting position on the ground, in the same manner as a Mallard. Whistling ducks, dabbling ducks, and most perching ducks are able to take flight directly. The steamer ducks, pochards, sea ducks and, stiff-tails typically run along the water surface for some distance before becoming airborne, and two species of steamer ducks are limited to "steaming" over the water surface with simultaneous wing-strokes and foot-paddling.

Walking on land has been achieved with varying degrees of success by waterfowl. The long-legged Magpie Goose and Spur-winged Goose walk admirably, and so to a more limited extent do some of the sheldgeese. The typical whistling ducks are capable walkers, though their large feet lend an air of awkwardness to them, while the swans are definitely out of their element on land. Among the true geese, the long-legged Hawaiian Goose is certainly the most proficient walker. The short-legged species of perching ducks and the dabblers all walk with a distinct waddle. The legs of pochards and most of the sea ducks are placed so far backward that the birds often assume a decided upright stance when walking. The feet of stiff-tails are situated so far aft that walking can be done only for short distances, and these birds rarely leave water.

Perching is achieved with facility only in a very few waterfowl. The Magpie Goose, with its long hind toe, perches easily. This ability is shared by the sharply clawed perching duck group, and to some extent by the whistling ducks. The hole-nesting sea ducks (such as goldeneyes) undoubtedly also perch occasionally, though apparently not with the frequency of the true perching ducks.

Social cooperative behavior between unpaired birds sometimes includes mutual preening or "nibbling." Such social preening is typical of the whistling ducks (especially the White-faced) and the Orinoco Goose, and also occurs between mated pairs in the North American Wood Duck, Mandarin Duck, and Andean Goose. Self-preening and bathing are very frequently performed by all waterfowl and are essential for the maintenance of waterproof plumage (Plates 6, 24, 113). The preening behavior functions partly to spread oil from the preen gland at the base of the tail over the plumage. Such behavior has the double effect of maintaining the feathers and preserving the surface condition of the bill and legs. Preening also maintains the interlocking and spacing structure of the feather barbs to prevent the entrance of water. All waterfowl perform these preening movements in the same manner, and even newly hatched birds exhibit exactly the same grooming movements as do adults, preening in the regions of the adult feather tracts as if these were already present. During molting, much time is spent by waterfowl in rubbing the bill edge over the body feathers to help loosen and discard old feathers. Preening movements are also used in various ways during sexual or threat displays by many waterfowl. These movements involve preening dorsally, breast-preening, and preening behind the wing (Figure 4).

Two kinds of wing-stretching movements are performed by all waterfowl, and in the same manner by all species. These movements include the wing-and-leg-stretch, in which one wing and the corresponding leg are extended laterally to the utmost (Plate 60), and the both-wings-stretch, during which the wings are raised in a partially extended position over the back while the head and neck are stretched forward. Stretching movements do not usually appear as displays, but the wing-and-leg-stretch forms a part of the precopulatory sequence of goldeneyes (Figure 4).

A frequent shaking movement of standing waterfowl is the general body-shake, which starts as a lateral shaking of the tail and progresses forward, ending with a vigorous headshake (Plate 5). This general shake has also been modified by several species of waterfowl to serve as a threat or sexual display, and as a swimming-shake it frequently serves as a preliminary or introductory phase of courtship activities (Figure 4).

When sleeping, waterfowl tuck their bills into the feathers between the bases of the wings in the manner typical of many birds (Plate 53). While resting, one leg is often tucked up into the flank feathers (Plate 18) or, in some swans, may be held up facing backward at the level of the tail. The White-backed Duck sometimes even rests its legs on the upper surface of the back.

In a few species the very interesting behavioral trait of carrying the young on the backs of the parents may be seen. This behavior is found in three species of swans; in order of decreasing frequency it occurs in Black-necked, Mute, and Black Swans (Plate 33). It also has been reported for the Musk Duck, Salvadori's Duck, and some other species of ducks. The young climb aboard from the flank region just in front of the tail, then huddle between the wing and scapular feathers, usually remaining almost entirely concealed except for an occasional peek out. Carrying is most frequently observed during the first week after hatching, when the young are weak and in need of frequent rest or brooding. In the Musk Duck at least, the young are said to clutch tightly to the neck or back feathers of the adult, thus enabling it to dive with the young aboard. It has even been reported by Australian observers that the female will sometimes take flight with the young on her back, especially when the breeding ponds begin to dry up and the birds must move to new water areas. Since it is known that the young do hang on very tightly, this seems entirely possible and would provide for this highly aquatic species a

FIGURE 4. General behavior patterns as illustrated by various ducks. Upper left: *Dorsal preening* by Surf Scoter. Upper right: *Preening the breast*, White-winged Scoter. Middle left: *Preening behind the wing*, Ringed Teal. Middle right: *Wing flapping*, Harlequin Duck. Lower left: *Swimming shake*, Steller's Eider. Lower right: *Stretching of wing and leg*, Barrow's Goldeneye.

more feasible means of moving the brood than walking overland. This behavior harks back to the old and now usually discredited story of mother ducks taking their young on the back or in the bill to bring them down from nesting holes or other elevated places. Such tales have cropped up in various parts of the world for numerous species, including the Northern Shelduck, North American Wood Duck, and the Common Goldeneye. It has, of course, been repeatedly observed that ducklings of such hole-nesting species as goldeneyes, Northern Shelducks, and North American Wood Ducks do typically jump out of the nesting hole in response to the female's calls, but this alternative means of moving the young should not be ridiculed and regarded entirely as disproven.

26. White-faced Whistling Duck

↑ **27.** Magpie Goose (pair)

↓ **28.** Spotted Whistling Duck

↑ 29. Lesser Whistling Duck (pair)   ↓ 30. Red-billed Whistling Duck (pair)

↑ 31. White-backed Duck (male)　　　　　　　　　　↓ 32. Mute Swan (male)

↑ 33. Black-necked Swan (carrying young)   ↓ 34. Bewick's Swan (family)

↑ 35. Coscoroba Swan (adult)　　　↓ 36. Lesser White-fronted Goose (pair)

↑ 37. Emperor Goose (female)

↓ 38. Cape Barren Goose (pair)

39. Hawaiian Goose (adult male)

40. Red-breasted Goose (pair)

↑ 41. Freckled Duck (adults)   ↓ 42. Blue-winged Goose (pair)

43. Magellan Goose (pair)

↑ 44. Orinoco Goose (grazing)   ↓ 45. Egyptian Goose (pair grazing)

↑ 46. Cape Shelduck (pair)   ↓ 47. Radjah Shelduck (pair)

↑ 48. Magellanic Flightless Steamer Duck   ↓ 49. Spur-winged Goose (pair)

↑ 50. Muscovy Duck (male)

↓ 51. Hartlaub's Duck (family)

52. Comb Duck (male)

Sound
Production

*B*OTH vocal and mechanical methods of sound production are used by waterfowl; of these the vocal method is by far the more important. It is probably true that no species of waterfowl is entirely mute, although the vocalizations produced range from the wheezy huffing of the male Muscovy Duck to the magnificent clarion calls of the Trumpeter Swan.

The Magpie Goose has a very ordinary gooselike voice produced by an extraordinary trachea, or "windpipe." This trachea, up to 50 inches long in an adult male, is convoluted between the breast muscle and the skin in a unique fashion. Although none of the other waterfowl has a trachea convoluted in this manner, similar examples occur in certain currasows, which are fowllike birds of the family Cracidae. The actual vocal organ, or syrinx, of Magpie Geese is very small in both sexes (Figure 5) and the most common adult call is a nasal honking note. A gooselike hissing is also uttered during nest defense. Magpie Goose goslings frequently utter mellow whistles, including a call that results in their being fed. Adult Magpie Geese are possibly the only waterfowl that regularly feed their precocial young from bill-to-bill, a trait reminiscent of rails, gulls, and various other birds. Juvenile Magpie Geese retain their whistling notes until they are about six months old, when gradually their voices change into the adult honking note.

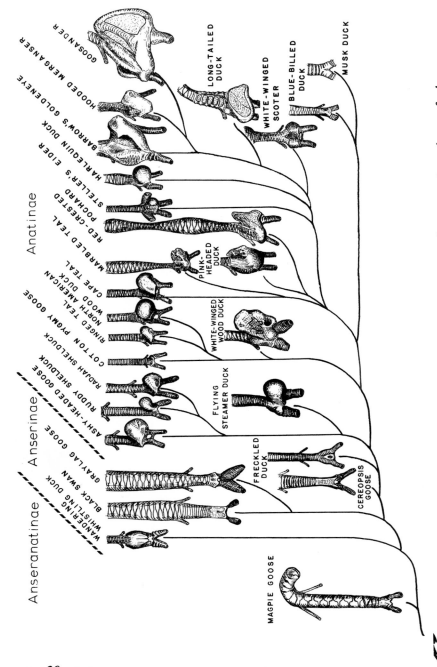

GOOSANDER

HOODED MERGANSER

BARROW'S GOLDENEYE

HARLEQUIN DUCK

STELLER'S EIDER

RED-CRESTED POCHARD

MARBLED TEAL

CAPE TEAL

NORTH AMERICAN WOOD DUCK

RINGED TEAL

COTTON PYGMY GOOSE

RADJAH SHELDUCK

RUDDY SHELDUCK

ASHY-HEADED GOOSE

GREYLAG GOOSE

BLACK SWAN

WANDERING WHISTLING DUCK

LONG-TAILED DUCK

WHITE-WINGED SCOTER

BLUE-BILLED DUCK

MUSK DUCK

PINK-HEADED DUCK

WHITE-WINGED WOOD DUCK

FLYING STEAMER DUCK

FRECKLED DUCK

CEREOPSIS GOOSE

MAGPIE GOOSE

Anatinae

Anserinae

Anseranatinae

FIGURE 5. Diagram of anatomical variations in the syrinxes of representative male waterfowl. One or more species of each tribe are shown, organized according to probable evolutionary relationships.

Whistling ducks are well described by their common name. All species have clear, sharp whistles in both sexes as adults, although Spotted Whistling Ducks also have a twanging, reedy, and less pleasant call. The whistled greeting calls, often uttered in flight, are beautiful and clear notes; the three-syllabled call of the White-faced Whistling Duck and the five- or six-noted call of the Red-billed Whistling Duck are among the most melodious. Besides these notes, the rapidly repeated and variably pitched notes uttered during threat are especially conspicuous. Male whistling ducks have a bulla, or a symmetrical bony enlargement at the base of the trachea, the shape of which varies somewhat in the different species (Figure 5). Females have considerably simpler tracheas, but it is apparently impossible to judge the sex of a bird by its call.

Three species of whistling ducks also have additional sound producers in the form of specialized outer primary feathers. In the Lesser Whistling Duck this consists of an unusual tongue-shaped extension of the outer vane that vibrates during flight and produces a whirring sound. The Spotted Whistling Duck lacks this distinct extension, but the outer part of the vane is much wider than the basal half, and so a flaglike shape results and a strong whirring noise is produced in flight. In the Wandering Whistling Duck the opposite arrangement is present, with the outer half of the vane strongly incised, and the basal part of normal width. In this species it is probable that the whole outer part of the primary vibrates and produces the marked whistling noise of the wings in flight.

Among the swans, by far the most remarkable voices and tracheas are possessed by the Whooper, Trumpeter, Whistling, and Bewick's Swans. In all these birds the trachea is convoluted inside the sternum or breastbone, increasing greatly the resonance of the call (Figure 6). These birds' penetrating notes are audible over great distances; the calls of the Trumpeter Swan can be heard well over a mile away. The other swans lack such elaborate tracheal specializations; the Black, Mute, and Black-necked Swans all have relatively weak voices. However, the Coscoroba Swan utters a fairly loud, ringing "Cos-cor-ooo." This call is made by both sexes, but the male's voice is higher pitched than that of the female. This sexual difference in pitch is also characteristic of all the true geese, including the Cape Barren Goose. Most swans as well as geese typically hiss when protecting their nests or young.

Males of nearly all species of sheldgeese have whistling notes that are frequently used in threat and sexual displays. The only exception is the male Egyptian Goose, which has an asthmatic breathing call reminiscent of a steam locomotive. Males of some species such as the Magellan Goose and Orinoco Goose also produce curious grunting noises during sexual display. Females of all the sheldgeese as well as the shelducks have low-pitched, ducklike, quacking voices. Most male shelducks have loud, honking voices, but male Radjah and Northern

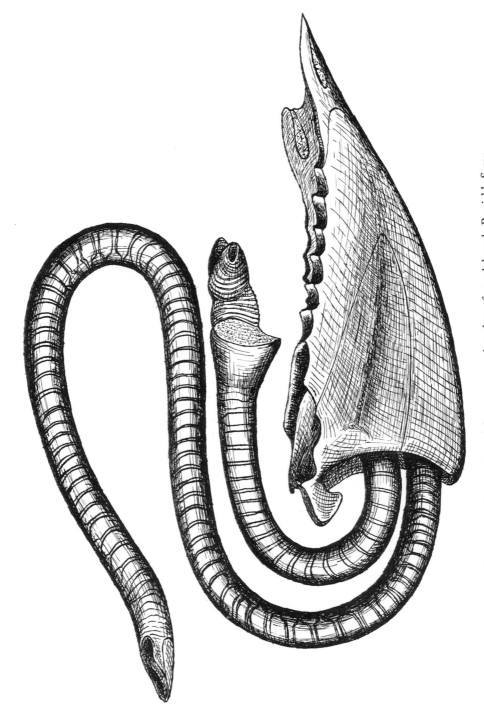

FIGURE 6. Lateral view of the sternum and trachea of an adult male Bewick's Swan.

Shelducks evidently utter only whistled notes. Males of these two species, as well as those of all the sheldgeese, have tracheas with large, bony bullas at the syrinx, where the bronchi branch to the lungs (Figure 5). In the Northern Shelduck there are inflations on both sides, but among the other shelducks and in the true ducks, only the left side is strongly inflated. Males of the shelduck species that possess honking voices have only very small bullas. However, male steamer ducks, whose calls range from rasping grunts to almost pure whistles, have tracheas with large, rounded bullas (Figure 5).

The means by which these structures operate still remains somewhat speculative, but presumably the bony sound chamber operates in much the same manner as a mechanical whistle, producing a whistling note as air is rapidly passed by it through the trachea. Female ducks, and males of species that lack such bullas, instead apparently rely on the vibration of the soft tympanic membranes located between the base of the trachea and the bronchi. These thin membranes are readily vibrated by the passage of air across them, and pitch apparently is regulated by varying the tension on the membranes through the use of two opposing pairs of muscles. In the geese and probably also in ducks, sound is evidently produced by inhalation as well as by exhalation, since the air sac in the region of the crop can frequently be observed to enlarge during calling.

VOCALIZATION OF TYPICAL DUCKS

As a group, the perching ducks show a wide variation in vocal abilities. Female Muscovy Ducks, Comb Ducks, and Spur-winged Geese all have weak calls uttered only during periods of great excitement. The voices of female Hartlaub's Duck and the White-winged Wood Duck are much louder and, during display, females will often call in concert with the males. The pygmy geese are characterized by having high-pitched whistles in the males and squeaking quacks in females. Female Ringed Teal, North American Wood Ducks, Mandarin Ducks, and Maned Geese also have very unusual voices; and of all the perching ducks, only the female Brazilian Teal might be said to produce a typical "quacking" call. Males of all these species have whistling voices that vary greatly in tone and quality. Except for pygmy geese, which have more simply constructed tracheas, all the male perching ducks have bony bullas of some sort (Figure 5).

Among the dabbling ducks there is also much vocal variation, but males of most species produce whistled notes of some kind, especially during pair-formation. Indeed, male wigeons have no calls other than whistles. Whistles are, however, lacking in the Baikal Teal, Silver Teal, Hottentot Teal, and all the "blue-winged" ducks (those with light blue upper wing coverts) except the Blue-winged Teal. The male Baikal Teal has a most unusual hollow-sounding clucking, and the male calls of the Silver Teal, Hottentot Teal, and Garganey are weak and curiously mechanical rattling notes. Similar but generally more nasal notes are uttered by males of the Cinnamon Teal and all the shovelers. The male Blue Duck has a sibilant whistle similar to that of wigeons, and male Torrent Ducks and Pink-eared Ducks also have penetrating whistling calls. In all the typical dabbling ducks, as well as in these "aberrant" species, males have tracheas with asymmetrical bony bullas (Figure 5). In two species of dabbling ducks there are also enlargements in the tracheal tube itself. Females of apparently all the typical dabbling ducks have characteristic quacking notes, termed "decrescendo calls," which usually descend in pitch. Other calls are also frequently produced by females of these species, especially during courtship display.

Voices in the pochard group are quite varied. Females usually have harsh growling calls and generally lack the "quacking" notes of female dabblers. The males typically have at least two distinct calls, both of which are used mainly during courtship. These usually include soft whirring or cooing notes that are not audible over great distances. However, the scaups and a few other species also utter rapid, mellow whistles. Males of all pochards have tracheas that are variably enlarged and always end in a large asymmetric bulla. This bulla is not rounded and entirely bony as in the dabbling ducks, but instead is angular and partially membranaceous (Figure 5). This latter feature possibly accounts for the mellow and soft qualities of most male pochard calls.

In the sea ducks, a striking variety of calls are found. Males of the larger species of eiders utter various dovelike cooing voices during their courtship displays. However, the male Steller's Eider is almost entirely silent during its display. Male Black and Surf Scoters possess wonderfully clear courtship whistles or liquid calls. The male White-winged Scoter, however, is reported to be relatively silent, sometimes uttering a bell-like note in flight. The Harlequin Duck is reputed to have high-pitched, mouselike piping notes in both sexes. It is in the Long-tailed Duck that the sea ducks find their vocal champion, for the male "Oldsquaw's" loud, yodeling calls carry an indelible air of wildness matched by few other birds.

The voices of male goldeneyes and mergansers vary so greatly that it is impossible to characterize them. Likewise, the male tracheal specializations of these sea ducks are bizarre in the extreme and almost defy description (Figure 5). Both the Barrow's and the Common Goldeneye have mid-tracheal swellings which in the latter species is conelike and telescoped. During the extreme head-throw displays of goldeneyes, these tracheas become extended momentarily, then return to the normal position. Males of both species of goldeneyes and the Black Scoter also have very narrow outer primary feathers that produce the characteristic whistling sounds these birds make in flight.

Although the sea ducks exhibit remarkable variability in their vocal capabilities, the stiff-tailed ducks exceed even them in originality. Males of almost all the species except the Maccoa Duck and the Musk Duck appear to lack any really effective syringeal sound production, but they have improvised in various ways. The White-headed Duck and North American Ruddy Duck have tracheal air sacs in the neck region which are inflated and beaten with the bill during the male's display, thus producing a soft drumming sound. The Argentine Ruddy Duck, Australian Blue-billed Duck, and perhaps also the Maccoa Duck can inflate the esophagus with air, and they all perform a remarkable water-slapping display with their necks fully inflated. The Black-headed Duck has an inflatable throat sac and the Musk Duck has a similar subgular pouch behind the expandable wattle, both of which may possibly modify sounds produced during their displays. Some of the male stiff-tails also kick up water with their feet; the male Musk Duck produces particularly loud and conspicuous splashes in conjunction with whistles that are audible over considerable distances.

Social
Behavior

CERTAINLY one of the most fascinating aspects of waterfowl behavior is that of social display. Although the term "display" includes all means of communication ("signals") which have been evolved by species to convey information between individual members, and thus includes their vocalizations, we shall here consider only primarily visual signals of social or sexual significance.

There are several types of such visual signals, which can be functionally classified as social integration displays, agonistic displays (those associated with attack and escape), and primarily sexual displays. These categories are somewhat subjective ones, and some signals clearly serve more than one of these functions.

It is probably accurate to say that most displays in waterfowl are primarily inherited or innate rather than learned. Some evidence for this is the fact that displays can often be elicited from newly hatched birds. Goslings of Magellan Geese will, for example, regularly perform the typical adult threat display of rearing back and calling when disturbed. Downy North American Ruddy Ducks have frequently been observed to perform the complex breast-drumming courtship display of adult males. As a greeting ceremony to their mother, South American Green-winged Teal ducklings perform the same gaping display used by adult males toward females during courtship. Newly hatched Common Eiders almost constantly perform the typical chin-lifting aggressive display of adults and, likewise, downy goldeneyes perform the same rotary head movements that are used by adults during courtship display. Downy young swans and geese often join in the *Triumph Ceremonies*[1] of their parents, even when only a few weeks old.

It thus appears that downies of both sexes may often perform displays that are limited to one sex in adults. By the injection of sex hormones it is also usually possible to initiate adult courtship displays among ducklings, further proving that these latent behavior patterns are potentially present in a fully developed state well before they are normally elicited.

Displays that might be regarded as social integration activities include such things as mutual preening and those displays associated with preflight behavior. Since waterfowl are for the most part gregarious and often cluster together, it is important that the entire family or flock become aware when one of their group is about to fly. This awareness is especially essential for the larger geese and swans, which usually require considerable room for their take-offs. Thus in most swans and geese, vocalizations form an important aspect of preflight behavior. A rapid lateral head-shaking is also typical of these birds in the preflight situation. In Canada Geese and Barnacle Geese the chin is strongly lifted during this head-shaking, and the flashing of the white throat markings provides a conspicuous signal to other birds. However, in the Mute, Black, and probably the Black-necked Swan there is no calling or head-shaking, and an imminent take-off is signaled by an alert posture, an erect neck and slimmed plumage, and a facing into the wind.

Magpie Geese usually shake their heads laterally before taking flight, but repeated calling is also an important signal. Whistling ducks shake their heads laterally, but usually do not call. Preflight movements in the shelducks and sheldgeese have not been well studied, but they appear to be mainly head-shaking and chin-lifting movements. Among the perching ducks, many species make rather slow, pointing movements of the head in the direction they are about to fly; but among the dabbling ducks, these head movements are more jerky and are often alternated with lateral head-shaking. Pochards perform rapid head-shaking and chin-lifting movements. Sea ducks lack such conspicuous signals, and instead assume an alert posture while facing into the wind, occasionally shaking the head laterally. Preflight movements in the stiff-tails are not well-known, but these birds only rarely take to flight, and it is probable that such signals are poorly developed in this group.

Agonistic displays, such as threat postures, are frequently observed in waterfowl. In the Mute, Black, and Coscoroba Swans one of these postures consists of the well-known threat display involving lifting of the folded wings, making the bird appear much larger than it actually is. Ruffling the scapular feathers and

[1] Names of specific displays are usually italicized or capitalized.

spreading the tail is another method of increasing apparent body size, and is often used by whistling ducks, geese, and females of many ducks when threatening or when defending the nest or young. Wing-flapping is employed as a threat display by several swans, and a shaking or alternate flicking of the folded wings is also performed by most geese and some swans during threat display. All the swans raise their neck feathers as a threat signal, but in the true geese the neck feathers are usually vibrated rather than erected. This behavior is rendered more conspicuous in many species by the vertically arranged furrows as, for example, in the Hawaiian Goose, or by lengthened nape feathers as in the Red-breasted Goose. Many species of ducks lift their chins slightly during threat display, and some, such as the Baikal Teal and Steller's Eider, have conspicuous black chin or throat patterns that are brought into view at such times.

Actual attack in waterfowl takes various forms. Birds usually swim or fly at one another, beating with the wings and grasping with the bill. The male Muscovy Duck even rears back and strikes both with its wings and its sharply clawed feet. Some sea ducks, steamer ducks, and the Musk Duck typically attack other ducks from under water in a highly effective manner. A few species, such as the Spur-winged Goose, have formidable sharp spurs on their wings that can cut an opponent to pieces; the shelducks and sheldgeese have similar bony protuberances that also make effective weapons. Except perhaps in these species, fights among waterfowl rarely lead to serious injury or death, although occasionally feathers may be lost during such encounters.

PAIR-FORMING DISPLAYS

Sexual displays in waterfowl can be roughly divided into "courtship" or pair-forming displays, pair-maintaining displays, and those displays directly associated with fertilization. Of these the first type is generally the most elaborate and uniquely characteristic of each species, since every one must have its own distinctive pair-forming rituals in order to prevent mismatings.

No obvious courtship display has been observed in the Magpie Goose, and the courtship of whistling ducks appears to be simple and quite similar to that of geese. In geese, the male courts the female by swimming ahead of her in a characteristic "haughty" posture, with the tail somewhat cocked and the head held high. Among both geese and swans, pairs seem to be firmly established through the repeated performance of the *Triumph Ceremony* between two birds. This display typically occurs after the male has threatened or attacked some intruder, and then returns to the female, calling excitedly. The female reciprocates his posturing and calling, and typically the two birds stand almost side by side, clamoring in each other's ears. However questionably attractive this behavior might seem to a

FIGURE 7. Sexual displays of waterfowl species representing various tribes. Upper left: Post-copulatory display of Fulvous Whistling Ducks. Upper right: Postcopulatory display of Barn-acle Geese. Middle left: *Preening-behind-the-wing* by male Northern Shelduck to female. Middle right: *Short-high-and-broad* display of male Flying Steamer Duck. Lower left: *Display shake* of male Mandarin Duck. Lower right: Postcopulatory *Bill-down* display of male Greater Scaup.

human, it has the desired effect of establishing a firm pair bond that will last indefinitely.

Courtship in the shelducks and sheldgeese tends to be more diversified and elaborate than in the true geese, although not quite so complex as in the rest of the ducks. In this group the male often alternately threatens any opponents, real or imaginary, and displays sexually to his mate or potential mate, usually with preening, wing-lifting, or strutting movements. The iridescent wing coloration of these birds is frequently exposed during such displays. In the Northern Shelduck there is also an actual preening display that specifically exhibits the speculum pattern (Figure 7). Female shelducks and sheldgeese are exceedingly aggressive birds and usually *Incite* their males to attack almost every animate object (Plate 54). If the male responds blindly and returns from the fray thoroughly beaten, it is quite frequent that the seemingly implacable female will promptly reject her mate and begin to court the victor, regardless of what species it may be!

It is among the perching ducks that some of the most beautiful male plumage patterns are to be found, particularly in the wing feathering. For example, the iridescent speculum patterns of the Brazilian Teal, Ringed Teal, North American Wood Duck, and Mandarin Duck are extraordinary. It is therefore not surprising that preening displays which flash these colors toward the female are particularly frequent in this group, especially in the last two species mentioned. Male perching ducks commonly perform displays consisting of exaggerated general shakes (Figure 7) and display drinking is likewise frequent in some perching ducks. Also important for some species is the male display called *Turning-the-back-of-the-head*. Females of many perching ducks *Incite* their mates against one another in the manner of shelducks, but actual fighting among these birds is infrequent except in the case of some larger species.

Among the dabbling ducks we are confronted with numerous species having elaborate male plumages and displays, and it is interesting that no two species of dabbling ducks breeding in the same region have exactly the same male plumage patterns and display repertoires. Many individual displays are, however, shared by numerous species of dabbling ducks, and Konrad Lorenz has given some of the most widespread male displays the descriptive names *Head-up-tail-up*, *Grunt-whistle*, and *Down-up*. Of these, the *Head-up-tail-up* is perhaps the most spectacular (Figure 8). It consists basically of a rapid, simultaneous jerking up of the head and tail, at the same time lifting the folded wings, momentarily flashing the speculum. A whistle is uttered at the peak of the display. The *Grunt-whistle* is equally remarkable, and consists of a rapid scooping up of water with the bill as it is quickly drawn toward the breast, uttering a whistle and throwing up an arc of droplets on the side toward the courted female, followed by a rearing up of the

FIGURE 8. Male pair-forming displays of representative dabbling ducks. Upper left: *Grunt-whistle* of Falcated Duck. Upper right: *Head-up-tail-up* of Northern Pintail. Middle left: *Down-up* of Bahama Pintail. Middle right: *Bridling* of South American Green-winged Teal. Lower left: *Burping* of Baikal Teal. Lower right: *Mock-feeding* of Australian Shoveler.

body and a shaking of the head and tail (Figure 8). In the *Down-up*, the male suddenly lifts its tail and submerges its breast as it performs a drinking movement toward the courted bird; in quickly raising its bill, it often throws up a little shower of water droplets and typically utters a whistled note (Figure 8).

A drawing back of the head along the back, called *Bridling*, is another of the numerous male displays of various dabbling ducks (Figure 8). Calling during vertical neck-stretching, or *Burping*, is performed by most male dabbling ducks (Figure 8). Males of most species also perform rapid *Preening-behind-the-wing*, exhibiting their beautiful speculum colors, and also *Turn-the-back-of-the-head* to *Inciting* females. Besides *Inciting*, females of many species perform a *Nod-swimming* display in which the head is lowered and usually nodded vigorously as the female swims rapidly past the males. In a few species, such as Mallards, the males also *Nod-swim*, usually linking it to the *Head-up-tail-up* display. Although practically all species of ducks perform drinking as an appeasement gesture, in the blue-winged ducks two other derivations of foraging movements, *Mock-feeding* and *Tipping-up*, occur as major male courtship displays (Figure 8).

Male courtship displays among the pochards are more uniform. Practically all species of pochards have *Head-throw* displays ranging from a rudimentary flicking of the bill to a point short of the vertical, as in Lesser Scaup, to those of the Redhead and Ring-necked Duck, in which the head actually momentarily touches the base of the tail. The call accompanying this display is usually a soft sound varying from a dovelike cooing note in Canvasbacks to a sharper whistle in some of the scaups. Essentially the same calls are uttered during a *Kinked-neck* posture. A second and distinctly different courtship note is usually uttered with a convulsive jerk of the wings and tail, giving the impression of a slight cough. This *Coughing* call is generally sharper than the preceding one and is sometimes a whistling note. Most of the male pochards also assume a posture called *Sneaking* in which the bird stretches his neck forward and points his bill toward a female or another male. This movement is usually accompanied by a call, and may function either as a threat to other males or a sexual display to females. Males of most species *Preen-behind-the-wing* and thus expose the gray or white speculum; often the rattling noise produced by the bill as it rubs over the feather quills can be heard for ten yards or more. Males frequently *Turn-the-back-of-the-head* to females, while lowering their forehead feathers to produce a very low-crowned appearance. Besides *Inciting*, females also *Preen-behind-the-wing* to apparently preferred males. In a few species both the female and the male perform the *Head-throw* and the *Kinked-neck* displays.

Male courtship displays of the sea ducks are so elaborate that they almost defy description. The males of the larger eiders perform various head-lifting movements while uttering soft and mellow cooing notes. They also turn their heads laterally, emphasizing the variably shaped or colored bill and the beautiful head feathering. *Wing-flapping* and an exaggerated version of the *Swimming-shake* are conspicuous displays of all the eiders, and in both cases the throat or abdominal patterns are probably displayed to the females (Figure 9). The smaller Steller's Eider shares a few display features with these larger birds, such as the *Swimming-shake* (*Upward-stretch*) and lateral *Head-Turning*, and a particularly rapid and striking *Rearing* display by which the brownish abdomen is momentarily flashed. The King Eider performs *Reaching* or *Pushing* head movements as it utters its cooing sounds and inflates its neck (Figure 9). A *Chest-lifting* display occurs in Surf Scoters, and the Black Scoter has a spectacular *Tail-snap* followed by a *Low Rush* over the water like a miniature hydroplane. One of the conspicuous displays of the Long-tailed Duck is the *Ah-har-lik* call (onomatopoetic), which is often accompanied by a rapid *Head-throw*. A similar call is given during the well-named *Rear-end Display* in which the head and neck are lowered out over the water as the hindquarters and tail are raised vertically. Little is currently known of the male displays of the Harlequin Duck, but evidently elaborate posturings are lacking.

Displays of the goldeneyes have been studied and described by several authors, including Benjamin Dane and M. T. Myres. The number and complexity of these displays can only be suggested here. For example, both goldeneye species perform displays which involve throwing the head backward, but whereas in the Common Goldeneye there is both a simple *Head-throw* and two distinct types of *Head-throw-kick* displays (Figure 9), the male Barrow's Goldeneye performs only a single *Head-throw-kick* display. Several other complex display postures occur in these species; the Common Goldeneye thus has certain unique male displays such as the *Bowsprit* and *Masthead*, to mention but two. Although the closely related Bufflehead lacks any head-throw displays, it has several male postures similar to those of goldeneyes as well as a unique *Folded-wings-lifted* display (Figure 9).

The mergansers are at least as diverse as the goldeneyes in their male displays, and perhaps more so. Several species have not yet been well studied, but the Hooded Merganser, Smew, and Red-breasted Merganser are all known to have elaborate male posturing and calls. *Crest-raising* by the Hooded Merganser is especially spectacular (Figure 9). The Hooded Merganser and Smew also perform head-throw displays something like those of goldeneyes, but the male Red-breasted Merganser has a bizarre sequence of movements that include the *Salute* and the following *Curtsy* (Figure 9). Many of the sea ducks perform display flights, during which the male makes short flights toward the female, typically landing near her with a splash. Females of most and perhaps all sea ducks perform *Inciting* displays, but these are extremely variable in their visual and vocal characteristics.

↑ 53. Ruddy Shelduck (female resting)   ↓ 54. Paradise Shelduck (female inciting)

↑ 55. Australian Shelduck (pair)   ↓ 56. Northern Shelduck (pair, male on right)

↑ 57. Falkland Flightless Steamer Duck   ↓ 58. White-winged Wood Duck (pair)

↑ 59. Cotton Pygmy Goose (male) ↓ 60. Brazilian Teal (male stretching)

↑ 61. North American Wood Duck (female and young)   ↓ 62. Chilean Torrent Duck (male)

↑ 63. Salvadori's Duck (male dabbling)   ↓ 64. African Black Duck (pair, male at rear)

↑ 65. Chiloé Wigeon (pair)   ↓ 66. American Wigeon (pair, male in front)

↑ 67. Falcated Duck (pair)   ↓ 68. Gadwall (male)

↑ 71. Gray Teal (pair dabbling)   ↓ 72. Chestnut Teal (family)

↑ 73. New Zealand Brown Teal (pair)   ↓ 74. Common Mallard (pair)

↑ 75. Hybrid Mallard x Pintail (males)   ↓ 76. American Black Duck (pair, male on right)

↑ 77. Yellow-billed Duck (pair)   ↓ 78. Spot-billed Duck (pair of Indian race)

↑ 79. Australian Black Duck (pair) ↓ 80. Philippine Duck (female and young)

↑ 81. Bronze-winged Duck (male)   ↓ 82. Northern Pintail (male)

↑ 83. Brown Pintail (South Georgia race)   ↓ 84. Bahama Pintail (male)

FIGURE 9. Male pair-forming displays of representative sea ducks. Upper left: *Folded-wings-lifted* display of Bufflehead. Upper right: *Head-throw-kick* of Common Goldeneye. Middle left: *Wing-flapping* of Spectacled Eider. Middle right: *Pushing* display of King Eider. Lower left: *Crest-raising* display of Hooded Merganser. Lower right: *Curtsy* display of Red-breasted Merganser.

Among the stiff-tails, the males' pair-forming displays are not so much beautiful as they are ludicrous, at least among those that have been well studied. Thus, male North American Ruddy Ducks are veritable clowns, with their blue bills, white cheeks, feathered "horns," and cocked tails. They inflate their necks to almost double normal size, raise their tails to what appears to be an impossible angle, and then rapidly beat their bills on their inflated necks. They produce in this way a soft drumming sound, force air out from between their breast feathers, and cause bubbles to form around the front of the body. The other typical stiff-tails also have displays involving tail-cocking and neck-inflating, but they usually differ in their head movements, producing splashing sounds in various ways. The females of this group seem to be the least receptive of all waterfowl in their response to the males' displays. For all their efforts, the males will usually receive only a sharp jab if they approach too closely. No definite *Inciting* has been noted in stiff-tails, but few of the species have yet been studied thoroughly.

PAIR-MAINTAINING DISPLAYS

Displays associated with pair-bond maintenance and with copulation in waterfowl are generally much more uniform and less elaborate than pair-forming displays. Pair-maintaining displays of waterfowl frequently involve such behavior as mutual preening, mutual drinking, or other mutual responses. Precopulatory behavior in whistling ducks consists of *Head-dipping*, *Bill-dipping*, or *Drinking* by the male or by both birds, but unless one is very well acquainted with whistling duck behavior, it is unlikely that he would recognize these movements as being anything other than those of normal foraging. Postcopulatory displays in most species of whistling ducks including the White-backed Duck consist of a vigorous *Step-dance*, in which both birds rise side by side, calling loudly and simultaneously raising the wing on the opposite side from the partner (Figure 7). However, the Black-billed and Red-billed Whistling Ducks lack such elaborate postcopulatory ceremonies; they also generally perform their mating on the shore or at the water's edge. In swans and true geese the precopulatory displays are practically the same in all species, consisting of a mutual *Head-dipping* sequence similar to bathing movements. In geese (particularly the males), the tail is generally tilted upward and the whole body is held high in the water between dipping movements. Postcopulatory displays are more variable, but in most species there is a mutual calling with outstretched neck, raised bill, and sometimes with lifted or even fully spread wings (Figure 7).

In the sheldgeese and shelducks a mutual *Head-dipping* performance is also the typical precopulatory sequence of most species. The postcopulatory display is likewise relatively uniform in these, consisting of mutual calling as the birds rear up in the water side by side, with each bird raising one wing in a *Wing-lifting* display that closely resembles the *Step-dance* of the whistling ducks. Among perching ducks the precopulatory displays generally consist of mutual *Head-dipping*, *Bill-dipping*, or *Head-pumping* movements, although several of the larger species seem to have few if any specific precopulatory displays. Postcopulatory displays are also fairly simple in this group, with the male usually calling one or more times, with or without any other more specific posturings. Mutual *Head-pumping* is the usual precopulatory display of all the typical dabbling ducks, and postcopulatory behavior in this group consists of calling on the part of the male, usually in conjunction with *Burping*, *Bridling*, or other specific postcopulatory postures. *Nod-swimming* is a typical part of the male postcopulatory displays in the Mallardlike ducks. Like the perching ducks, female dabbling ducks usually simply bathe after copulation.

Head-pumping is either absent or is a minor part of the precopulatory displays of pochards, and instead both birds typically perform a sequence of *Bill-dipping*, *Drinking*, and dorsal *Preening* movements. Following treading, the male calls once and then swims away in a characteristic *Bill-down* posture (Figure 7). The female may swim for a time in the same position, but often begins to bathe immediately.

Unlike most of the preceding groups, precopulatory behavior in the sea ducks is marked by the female's assuming a flat, or prone, posture on the water as the male begins his precopulatory displays. These vary greatly, but often consist of displays associated with courtship plus others that occur only in the precopulatory situation, such as ritualized stretching, shaking, and preening movements. *Drinking* is a particularly common precopulatory display in goldeneyes, mergansers, and possibly other sea ducks. While the male is performing these displays, the female watches intently from her prone posture. Males of some species, such as the goldeneyes and Hooded Merganser, have certain rigid sequences of behavior that they invariably perform before mounting, but among others no specific sequence is obvious. In a few sea ducks such as the eiders, Smew, and Surf Scoter, the male normally performs one of his courtship displays as soon as treading is completed, and in many species a special postcopulatory display or a stereotyped retreat from the female occurs.

The Ruddy Duck is as yet the only typical stiff-tailed duck for which copulatory behavior has been well observed. The male repeatedly dips his bill in the water and then rapidly flicks it from side to side as he swims near the female, who usually does not assume a prone posture. After treading he performs his breast-drumming, or *Bubbling*, display several times to the female. Evidently the Musk Duck mates indiscriminately with any females that are attracted to its varied displays.

Although it is often difficult to understand how such a number and variety of elaborate displays as occur in the waterfowl have evolved, it is generally held that all displays have their origin as a result of conflicting tendencies to attack, escape from, or react sexually toward another bird. Thus, courting males are simultaneously driven toward attacking and fleeing from rival males and behaving sexually toward females, while females are caught in the similar dilemma of attacking, escaping from, and being sexually attracted to males. The *Inciting* behavior of female ducks, for example, clearly represents alternations of aggressive and escape (or appeasement) gestures. Drinking is used as an appeasement gesture by many waterfowl, and various displays by both sexes are often preceded or followed by drinking. *Turning-the-back-of-the-head*, thus hiding the bill, is an appeasement gesture found in various groups of birds and commonly performed by males to females in waterfowl.

If displays are motivated by a conflict of tendencies, what then are the actual raw materials of display motor patterns? In waterfowl there appear to be two major sources—ambivalent or compromise "intention" movements, and body maintenance or comfort movements. Thus, a female dabbling duck having conflicting motivations to attack and escape may gape, ruffle her scapular feathers, and spread her tail (postures of aggression), but also simultaneously withdraw her head into her shoulders (an escape gesture), all these intention movements combining to produce the distinctive *Gesture of Repulsion* display.

It is also common for male courtship and threat displays in waterfowl to be derived from apparently irrelevant responses, especially body maintenance or comfort movements. Thus, the general body-shake is utilized by various swans as a threat display. The swimming-shake is modified by numerous perching ducks, dabbling ducks, and sea ducks into a male courtship display, and by some sea ducks into a precopulatory display. Wing-flapping is also incorporated by some swans and the Andean Goose into a threat display, is employed by certain perching ducks and dabbling ducks as a courtship display, and occurs in a few sea ducks as a precopulatory display. Preening has been incorporated into a threat display by many perching ducks, dabbling ducks, and pochards; into some courtship displays by several of these same species; and into precopulatory displays by the pochards and some sea ducks. Vertical wing-stretching is possibly used as a threat display in Spur-winged Geese and wing- and leg-stretching is definitely the basis for a precopulatory display in goldeneyes.

Some waterfowl pair-forming displays exhibit behavior associated with aggression or warning followed by an apparent courtship or appeasement gesture. Examples include the *Chin-lifting* display followed by *Burping* and *Drinking* in Baikal Teal, and the linking by some pochards of the apparently aggressive *Sneak* posture with a subsequent *Kinked-neck* call. Precopulatory behavior is rich in displays derived from probable appeasement gestures such as drinking and apparently irrelevant behavior such as bathing and preening.

Breeding
Biology

*A*LTHOUGH gregarious throughout most of the year, waterfowl do not breed together in colonies as a general rule. Colonial nesting is probably most closely approached in artificially protected areas where such nesting is encouraged by human protection. Dense nesting colonies of Mute Swans, Black Swans, and Common Eiders have developed in some areas under these conditions. Similar semicolonial nesting occurs where suitable or safe nesting sites are restricted, as for example when Gadwalls, Canada Geese, and other species nest on small islands.

A far more general situation in waterfowl is the scattering of nests, the distance between the nests being partly determined by the species' territorial tendencies. In waterfowl, territoriality is perhaps most clearly apparent in swans, which under natural conditions normally build their nests in isolated surroundings. Most geese also are reputed to be relatively territorial, but offspring from a family often return to nest near their own place of hatching, and so family groups may develop rather high nesting densities in an area. Shelducks and sheldgeese are among the most aggressive of all waterfowl, which helps to explain why their nesting concentrations are normally sparse. The specialized nest requirements of shelducks, as well as other hole- or crevice-nesting ducks, further tend to reduce nesting concentrations of these birds. In the dabbling ducks, pochards, and ground-nesting sea ducks, the nest-site requirements are more general, and as a result it is possible for greater numbers of birds to nest in a particular location. H. A. Hochbaum concluded that water, a loafing spot, adjacent or nearby nesting cover, and food are the requisites for a suitable breeding territory in prairie-nesting ducks. The nest may be built some distance away from the water, and loafing spots are apparently less important to pochards than to dabbling ducks. Lyle Sowls has enlarged this breeding territory concept to include the home range, which consists of all the area occupied by a pair but not necessarily defended by the drake.

Exactly what aspect of the territory is actually defended is a debatable point. There is no doubt that among ducks at least the female is the primary focal point of defense, although she is usually not considered part of the territory ("a defended area"), as commonly defined. Territorial defense in waterfowl has therefore become greatly confused with the defense of the female, with attempted rape of other females, and with actual courtship flights. Several writers, such as Alex Dzubin, T. Lebret, and various German workers, have attempted to classify the types of chases commonly observed in ducks. My own conclusions, based on personal observations as well as those of these authors, are that pursuit flights and courtship flights are the two major kinds of chases that occur.

PURSUIT FLIGHTS

These usually occur when a second male lands near a mated pair and approaches the female. The female *Incites* her mate against him, and the intruding drake will often be threatened and possibly attacked by the female's mate. More often, however, the strange male forces the hen to take flight, following closely at her tail. The mated drake may take off behind the leading two and follow them at some distance, usually ignoring his mate's *Inciting* calls. The female attempts to elude the intruding drake, who may at times approach her so closely that he is able to grasp her tail or rump feathers, force her to the ground, and rape her. Usually, however, the intruding drake abandons the chase and the mated pair returns to their pond. This kind of chase has been called the "three-bird chase" as well as "territorial defense," the latter interpretation being most readily made when a drake of a mated pair takes off to chase a female (with or without her mate present) who happens to fly near his loafing area. After a short chase he generally abandons the flight and returns to his loafing spot. Lebret called such flights "expulsion flights," and whether they should be called this or regarded as "attempted rape flights" obviously depends on the intentions of the chasing male, which might change from expulsion to rape during the course of the flight. Sometimes other unmated or mated drakes observing the chase may also join in, but flights involving numerous drakes are usually of the next type. The presence of the female's

Inciting and the lagging of one drake provide the best recognition basis of such flights, which are frequent in Common Mallards, Northern Pintails, Gadwall, American Wigeon, and other dabbling ducks. I have also observed rape or attempted rape in whistling ducks, pochards, eiders, and even some geese.

When the female is involved in incubating or, perhaps already brooding, these pursuit flights take a different form. Since her mate has by this time usually deserted her, she does not *Incite* against an intruding male, but rather threatens him. In Common Mallards and many other dabbling ducks, this posture and call is termed the *Gesture of Repulsion* and consists of a grating call, spread tail, ruffled scapulars, gaping bill, and retracted head. Males seem to realize that such females are unprotected and press their attempts to rape to a greater degree than with mated females. The female is soon forced to take flight, a flight usually characterized by towering climbs and frequent "braking" by the female in her frantic efforts to escape, as well as by the frequently repeated *Gesture of Repulsion*. In such chases other drakes very often join in, and soon the female is exhausted and forced to the ground or water where she is then raped. Sowls suggested this behavior functions as a kind of "renesting courtship" for females that have lost their first clutch, ensuring the fertility of any second clutch that might be laid. These pursuit flights are very common in Common Mallards, Northern Pintails, and Red-crested Pochards, and also occur less commonly in other dabbling ducks and pochards.

COURTSHIP FLIGHTS

Courtship flights tend to occur earlier in the season than do the chases just described and are apparently only aerial versions of aquatic courtship. In my view, the female does not purposely take flight to initiate these maneuvers, but rather is frightened or forced into flight by the press of several males. The female is rapidly followed by from two to ten or more drakes, all of which remain as close as possible to her, uttering their courtship notes repeatedly. The female may *Incite* during these flights, particularly if she has formed a partial pair bond with one of the males. Occasionally two or more females are in these flights, but one is usual. The flights are beautiful and fascinating exhibitions of flying skill, and during late winter or early spring may be readily observed in many species of dabbling ducks, pochards, and probably others. It has been suggested that the flights serve to display the males' speculum patterns to the females, but this seems somewhat questionable. H. A. Hochbaum has observed aerial tail-pulling of the female by the males among Canvasbacks, Redheads, and Lesser Scaup; whether this is a part of aerial display or is similar to the tail-pulling during attempted rape chases is uncertain. Males of many of the sea ducks, as well as such dabbling ducks as Northern Shovelers, also have short display flights to the female during aquatic display activity. The purpose of such flights, called *Jump-flights*, *Short-flights*, and the like seems to be to draw attention to specific males and to put them in a better courting position in relation to the female.

PAIR FORMATION

The process of actual pair-bond development in waterfowl has been only inadequately studied. Probably the normal period of pair formation is rather extended, perhaps occurring over a period of several weeks or months. In geese this pairing apparently usually occurs during the second winter of life, and among Canada Geese up to a third of the females may nest when two years old. Recent observations on Trumpeter Swans indicate that pair formation may begin when the birds are only twenty months old, and nesting by females of this species may occur as early as two years and nine months after hatching. Pairs in geese and swans are evidently permanent, normally lasting for life. If one of the pair dies, however, a new mate is often taken by the remaining bird. Some instances of polygyny, or the mating of a male with several females, has been reported among swans and geese in confined situations, or where a shortage of males exists.

In the true ducks which mate every year, there is probably little remating with the same individuals, owing to the break-up of pairs in late spring, the high annual mortality rate, and a general shuffling of flocks during migration. Pair-formation in these species is closely tied to the process of female *Inciting*. In courting parties, females *Incite* "chosen" males against other males. Except in the shelducks, there is little overt effect on males by *Inciting*, for the preferred male's usual response is not to attack the other males, but rather to swim ahead of the female and *Turn-the-back-of-the-head* toward her. In so doing he exhibits in a symbolic way his acquiescence to her, and in some species the males have special nape patterns that are displayed at this time. Eventually the two birds separate from the courting flocks and thereafter avoid unpaired drakes, which may try to rape paired females.

Actual copulation, or treading, often appears to have little importance in the formation of waterfowl pairs. Treading is sometimes attempted by immature geese, but is usually not completed. In ducks, especially the dabbling ducks, treading occasionally begins in the fall well before pairs are formed and at least among Mallards may occur between relative "strangers." Since the male's gonads do not actively begin producing sperm until the days begin to increase in length, these fall copulations among Mallards are nonfunctional. No waterfowl are known to be regularly polygamous, although this has been recently reported for the Maccoa Duck. Some species such as the Musk Duck do appear to lack pair bonds, however, and pair bonds appear to be generally weak among the stiff-tailed ducks.

Of special interest is the Black-headed Duck, which is believed to be completely parasitic, laying its eggs in other birds' nests. Apparently its normal hosts are various South American species of ducks and especially coots, but females appear to be quite indiscriminate in their selection of suitable foster parents, and occasionally they may even drop eggs in the nests of ground-nesting hawks!

Nest sites usually appear to be chosen by the female among ducks, although the male frequently accompanies the female on her nest-hunting forays. Often the same exact site is used year after year. Among species nesting in cavities, the male sometimes inspects potential sites with the female, and occasionally even seems to "show" the female possible nesting sites.

NESTING

Nest-building may be done by the female or by both sexes; but only rarely does the male do the majority of the work. All waterfowl apparently lack the ability to carry nesting material in the bill. They simply reach out to the maximum extent of their necks, pick up material, and drop it back over their shoulders. By standing at various distances from the nest site, material is thus gradually accumulated in sufficient quantities to form a nest. A few waterfowl such as eiders and Brant, use practically no natural nesting materials, the nest consisting almost entirely of down and feathers (Plate 21). Others, such as the Magpie Goose, whistling ducks, and the White-backed Duck, use little or no down whatsoever. This latter situation is typical of only those species in which both sexes incubate and the eggs are never left. In the Magpie Goose both sexes build the nest, and the same is probably true of whistling ducks. Magpie Geese sometimes construct several preliminary "stages," or "dummy nests," before building the actual nest. In the case of swans and true geese both sexes help build the nest, and in some (the Cape Barren Goose, for example) the male often does the major part of the building.

Nest-building may be started a considerable time before the first egg is laid. I once observed a Cape Barren Goose pair at the Wildfowl Trust that began working on a nest forty days before the first egg was laid. This time is usually much less; I also observed that a Trumpeter Swan laid her first egg eight days after the nest was begun, and five to ten days is perhaps an average figure for geese. However, arctic-nesting Snow Geese may lay their first eggs a few days after their arrival, as soon as the nest site is free of snow.

Egg-laying is usually done in early morning. Most if not all ducks lay every day, so that a typical clutch of eight or more eggs can be completed in a week or two. In probably all swans (Coscoroba uncertain), eggs are laid regularly every other day, and five to six eggs is a usual clutch. Some arctic geese such as Ross'

Goose lay eggs at daily intervals, but most geese also lay every other day. At least some of the "black geese" (*Branta*) and possibly some of the sheldgeese average about one and a half days between eggs. This latter interval is also typical of the Magpie Goose, which usually lays in early mornings and late afternoons alternately. The female Magpie Goose may come to the nest some time before actually laying, and the act of laying appears to be rapidly performed. The bird merely rears back slightly for a second or two as the egg is deposited, then settles down again.

During the period of egg-laying the nests of most waterfowl are often left unattended, and the eggs of such exposed nests are merely covered with feathers and down. In some cases, down is not added before three or four eggs are present. Incubation does not begin until the laying of the last or sometimes the penultimate egg, thus the young all hatch at approximately the same time. In the White-backed Duck and at least some other whistling ducks the male does most of the incubation. It is common for one sex to incubate by day and the other by night, at least this is true among species in which both sexes incubate. In the Magpie Goose, at least, the male usually sits at night. Most incubating waterfowl pluck down from their lower breast to help insulate the eggs, since "incubation patches" are not formed in waterfowl by feather loss through hormonal action.

Nest-relief ceremonies are performed by some of the species in which both sexes normally incubate, such as the Magpie Goose, Black Swan, and Mute Swan. In these species the relieving bird swims or walks up to the nest, calling frequently. These calls are typically answered by the sitting bird. The approaching bird then climbs up on the nest and sometimes literally pushes the other bird off. Before the latter leaves the nest, both usually perform nest-building movements. In the cases where only the female incubates she periodically leaves the nest for short periods to feed, although in a few species, such as the Common Eider, the female has been reported to fast for all of the four-week incubation period, leaving its nest every few days only long enough to obtain a drink of water.

In many waterfowl species, the female usually remains on the nest during the first day after hatching, and it is at this time that the young birds become "imprinted" on the parent. That is, they learn in a very rapid and almost irreversible manner the features by which their parent may be recognized and followed. When waterfowl eggs are hatched artificially, it is very easy to "imprint" newly-hatched birds, especially goslings, on artificial parents such as human beings, other birds, or even inanimate objects. The nest is generally left the second morning, although in geese and swans the family may return to it again at night for brooding. Downy waterfowl have a sufficient amount of reserve fat to keep them alive for several days without food, although they normally begin to forage within a few hours after hatching.

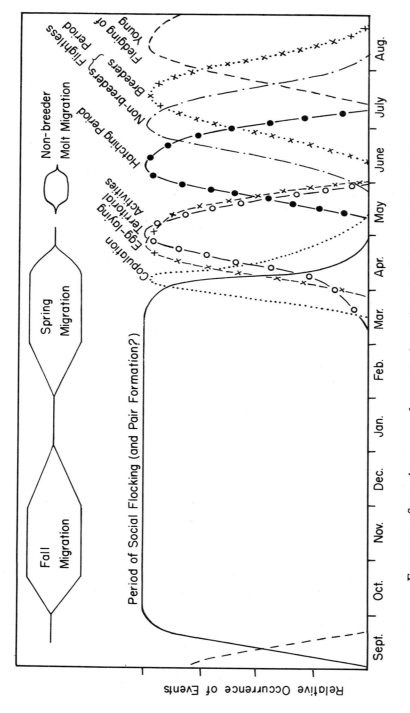

FIGURE 10. Seasonal sequence of events in the yearly cycle of the "Giant" Canada Goose, based on a composite of data from the northern United States and southern Canada.

Upon reaching water, families of most species tend to remain closely intact, but under crowded conditions there is often some intermixing of broods. All young waterfowl, regardless of species, feed to a large degree on aquatic insects and other invertebrate life during their period of most rapid growth. In some species, such as the steamer ducks, the young tend to flock together in large "crèches" after they are old enough to fend for themselves.

Although most adult ducks molt before they migrate to their wintering areas, in several species at least a partial migration occurs before molting. The "molt-migration" of the Northern Shelduck, from England and Scandinavia to the North Sea and other areas to undergo their molt, has been well studied. This migration of adults is carried out before the young are able to fly, and so these young birds frequently band together into large groups and leave for their wintering grounds at a later time. Summer migrations of male ducks to molting areas in certain Canadian lakes have been noted, similar movements have been seen in the United States, and large concentrations of molting male King Eiders have also been observed on the west coast of Greenland. Thousands of non-breeding "Giant" Canada Geese evidently fly north to the Keewatin tundra to molt. In Alaska, Steller's Eiders fly to the Alaska peninsula where, in such places as Izembek Bay, they congregate in the tens of thousands to molt. A few cases of molting after the arrival of ducks on their wintering areas in India have also been observed, and recently flightless female Gadwalls have been found on wintering grounds in Louisiana.

BREEDING CYCLES

It is interesting to consider how much time is involved in a successful breeding cycle for waterfowl. The Trumpeter Swan might normally need about ten days for building a nest, twelve days for laying a clutch of six eggs, thirty-six days for incubation, and approximately 120 days for the rearing of the young to the point of fledging, or roughly six months from the time of starting a nest until the young are on the wing. This represents the maximum possible breeding cycle length for a temperate or subarctic species, and renesting would clearly be impossible. At the other extreme, by starting their nesting as early as possible, some small arctic geese (Brant, Cackling Canada Geese) can breed in regions having scarcely two snow-free months.

The small Canada Geese that nest near Eskimo Point, Northwest Territories, collectively complete their egg-laying and incubation in only 38 to 40 days from the time of the first nest initiation, and no renesting is attempted after clutches have been completed. By comparison, Canada Geese that nest in California exhibit a more protracted nesting period of between 65 and 83 days, and

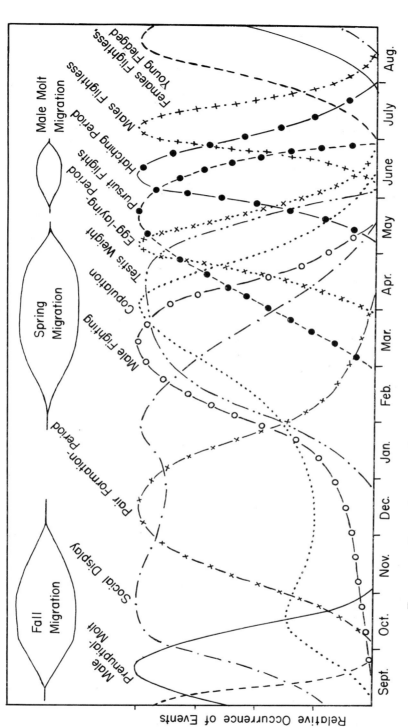

FIGURE 11. Seasonal sequence of events in the yearly cycle of the Mallard, based on a composite of data from northern Europe, southern Canada, and the northern United States.

individuals of these southern populations will often attempt to renest after a completed clutch has been destroyed. Furthermore, the large races of Canada Geese have significantly longer incubation and fledging periods than do the arctic-breeding populations, and require a minimum period of nearly four months to complete their breeding activities (Figure 10). Even the temperate-breeding Common Mallard can ill afford to waste any time after it arrives on its breeding grounds from its winter quarters, for it needs minimally an approximate eleven-week incubation and fledging time span that consumes a large part of the available breeding period in the northern portions of its range (Figure 11).

It is interesting that the length of the incubation period is only slightly correlated with the size of the adult bird. For example, the tiny Ringed Teal has an incubation period of 29 days, whereas some of the smaller arctic geese such as the Ross', Red-breasted, and the Cackling Canada Goose have periods of from 21 to 24 days (Table 2). It is also generally true that those species nesting in such relatively safe locations as tree holes have fairly long incubation periods relative to egg and body size, and those which nest in more exposed sites often have relatively shorter incubation periods. Apparently the shortest waterfowl incubation period is the 18–20 days for the Hottentot Teal (but the Wildfowl Trust reports it is 23 days), while the longest periods of from 36 to 40 days are those of the Trumpeter and Whooper Swans.

Species normally nesting in holes and crevices usually have whitish nest down, whereas those nesting in exposed places have down that is darker and more

TABLE 2

INCUBATION PERIODS OF VARIOUS WATERFOWL

Species or Group	Days
Magpie Goose	28–30
Whistling Ducks	26–30 (White-backed Duck 31)
Swans	34–40
True Geese	24–30 (Ross' Goose 21–23)
Sheldgeese and Shelducks	28–30
Perching Ducks	28–32 (Brazilian Teal 25; Muscovy Duck 35)
Dabbling Ducks	21–28 (Hottentot Teal 18–20; Crested Duck 30)
Pochards	23–29
Sea Ducks	25–30 (Bufflehead 22; Goosander and Harlequin Duck 30–32)
Stiff-tailed Ducks	21–27 (Musk Duck and Black-headed Duck unknown)

concealing in color. The female's nesting down is also sometimes of a different color from that worn during the nonbreeding period. Downy young vary greatly in coloration, but even those that are brightly patterned blend remarkably well into the background when they hide. Ruddy Ducks are extremely precocial, and within a few days after hatching the ducklings can remain under water while feeding for periods of as long as ten or fifteen seconds. These strong youngsters soon become independent, often leaving their mother after a week or two. Whether the reputed devotion of male Ruddy Ducks to their families is the result of any actual parental tendencies is doubtful; more probably it represents a prolonged sexual attraction of the male toward the female, even though the latter seems to pay little attention to the male's advances toward her.

In a few species of ducks, the male does actively assist the female in rearing and protecting the young. This is the usual situation in shelducks and in various southern hemisphere dabbling ducks including the Chiloé Wigeon, South American Green-winged Teal, Chestnut Teal, Cape Teal, Torrent Duck, and a few others. Probably the prolonged or irregular breeding seasons in these areas make advantageous a relatively continued attachment between the sexes.

In the last thirty years, and particularly since the publication of H. A. Hochbaum's *Canvasback on a Prairie Marsh*, many significant studies have been conducted on the breeding biology of various North American waterfowl. These include studies on the Ring-necked Duck (H. L. Mendall), Trumpeter Swan (W. E. Banko), American Black Duck (B. S. Wright), and various other dabbling ducks (L. K. Sowls). These and other works have provided a great deal of information on the behavioral and ecological aspects of nesting, incidence of renesting, predation effects, and the development of the young—to mention but a few aspects of their work.

Similar work in other countries has not developed so rapidly, but H. J. Frith's studies of the ecology of ducks in inland Australia have proved most interesting. Dr. Frith found that species such as the Musk Duck, Blue-billed Duck, and Black Swan which inhabit relatively permanent and stable water areas tend to have regular breeding seasons, whereas nomadic species clearly have no set season. These latter include such species as the Gray Teal and Pink-eared Duck. Unlike northern hemisphere species, whose internal sexual cycle is primarily regulated by changes in day-length as spring advances, these Australian species have instead synchronized their internal cycles to the fluctuations in water levels. For the Gray Teal a rise in water levels results in immediate sexual activity and egg-laying about a week to ten days later. In the Pink-eared Duck, however, sexual activity does not begin until the water levels have risen sufficiently to flood low-lying lands adjacent to the lagoons. At the same time the increased water results in increased reproduction in aquatic insects, and so the ducklings' food supply becomes greatest about the time of hatching (Plate 98). Plankton supplies, needed by the ducklings of the Pink-eared Duck, increase more slowly than insect populations; thus, synchrony of hatch and food supply in this species is achieved by a relatively slower development of the Pink-eared Duck's gonads. The Freckled Duck appears to have a somewhat more regular breeding season, but it can also breed at other favorable times when flooding occurs. It thus seems to represent an intermediate condition of adaptability to irregular breeding opportunities.

Another fascinating study in the ecology of waterfowl breeding has been provided by Graham Cooch, who has studied the breeding colonies of Snow Geese in the Canadian arctic. Dr. Cooch discovered that the "blue" phase of the Snow Goose has slightly different ecological tolerances regarding nesting time, and that white-phase birds tend to nest earlier than blue-phase birds. However, predation and other forms of nesting loss such as flooding are greatest early in the season. In a normal season, therefore, blue-phase birds would be favored. However, if a season is extremely retarded, a higher proportion of white-phase birds succeed in rearing young, because of a more widely spread nesting curve. Thus, both phases are more successful in early nesting seasons than late ones, but blue-phase or mixed pairs are generally more successful than white-phase birds, except in extremely late seasons. As a result, there has been an increase in the occurrence and geographic range of blue-phase, which is favored by the relatively mild climatic conditions now prevailing in the arctic.

The breeding biology of most South American species of waterfowl is poorly known, and several species still deserve to be more fully investigated. One of these, the Torrent Duck of the Andes, is of special interest. This remarkable species lives in the fastest mountain streams of the Andes from Venezuela to Tierra del Fuego (Plate 91). Only a few nests have been found, and these have been located in crevices, recesses, or kingfisher burrows. Evidently the birds typically lay only two or three eggs, which are remarkably large compared with the adult female. The incubation period is still unknown, but the young are highly precocial and evidently take to the rapid streams shortly after hatching. Unlike most ducks, the male remains closely with the family, and carefully guards the young. Presumably the ducklings consume the same food as the adults, aquatic insect larvae, but this fact has not been determined. In Colombia, Peru, and Bolivia, I have observed families of Torrent Ducks and found that both adults and ducklings are readily able to negotiate rapids and small falls while escaping from danger. Fledglings frequently hide among the rocks along the river edges, and adults may even resort to crawling behind waterfalls where they are effectively hidden by the cascading water. The slim-bodied adults are also able to move upstream in what would appear to be impossible currents, using only the feet for locomotion. It has been suggested that the Torrent Duck is a highly specialized dabbling duck that, like the Salvadori's Duck of New Guinea, has been adapted

↑ 85. African Pygmy Goose (pair)   ↓ 86. Ringed Teal (family)

↑ 87. North American Wood Duck (male)   ↓ 88. Mandarin Duck (pair)

↑ 89. Australian Wood Duck (pair)   ↓ 90. Brazilian Teal (pair)

↑ 91. Chilean Torrent Duck (male)　　　　　　　　　↓ 92. Blue Duck (male)

↑ 93. European Wigeon

↓ 94. Baikal Teal (males)

↑ 95. Cape Teal (pair)　　　　　　　　↓ 96. Laysan Teal (female and young)

↑ 97. Crested Duck (pair)　　　　　　　　　↓ 98. Pink-eared Duck [TOM LOWE]

↑ 99. Marbled Teal (pair)   ↓ 100. Red-crested Pochard (male)

↑ 101. Redhead (pair) ↓ 102. Tufted Duck (female and young)

↑ 103. Greater Scaup (male)

↓ 104. Common Eider (American race)

↑ 105. King Eider (pair) ↓ 106. Spectacled Eider (male preening)

↑ 107. Steller's Eider · ↓ 108. Long-tailed Duck (male)

↑ 109. Black Scoter (European race)

↓ 110. Bufflehead (male)

↑ III. Common Goldeneye (male) ↓ II2. Hooded Merganser (male)

↑ 113. Goosander (pair)   ↓ 114. Black-headed Duck (male)

↑ 115. North American Ruddy Duck   ↓ 116. Musk Duck (male in foreground)

to stream-dwelling. However, behavioral evidence suggests that the Torrent Duck is much less like the other dabbling ducks than is the Salvadori's Duck, and probably should be regarded as a distinct tribe of waterfowl. In any case, its anatomical similarities to the Salvadori's Duck are almost certainly the result of convergent evolution to similar habitats, and the Torrent Duck is probably evolved from a perching duck ancestor rather than from the dabbling duck group.

Because of the relatively high mortality rate existing in wild populations, most waterfowl that survive to fledging do not live long enough to breed more than once or twice. Banding data indicate that first-year mortality rates among wild ducks may average about 50 per cent, or even higher. Older birds may be somewhat less vulnerable to hunting, but there evidently is little if any actual reduction in average mortality rates as waterfowl mature. Nonetheless, a few individual birds may reach remarkably old ages, as indicated by the recovery of a small number of very old banded wild waterfowl. Captive waterfowl may also survive to surprisingly old ages, as indicated in Table 3.

TABLE 3

SOME LONGEVITY RECORDS FOR WATERFOWL

Species	Maximum Age in Years	
Magpie Goose	26	(captivity)
Wandering Whistling Duck	$15\frac{1}{4}$	(captivity)
Trumpeter Swan	$32\frac{1}{2}$	(captivity)
Whistling Swan	19	(captivity)
Graylag Goose	26	(captivity)
Canada Goose	33	(captivity);
	23	(wild)
Egyptian Goose	25	(captivity)
Northern Green-winged Teal	20	(wild)
Common Mallard	20	(captivity);
	16	(wild)
Canvasback	19	(captivity)
European Pochard	20	(captivity; fertile entire period)
Redhead	$16\frac{1}{2}$	(captivity)
Common Goldeneye	17	(wild)

It may be seen that waterfowl have the potential of very long lifespans, although there is no evidence that any ever approach one hundred years of age, as sometimes is stated in popular literature.

Molts and Plumages

*A*LL waterfowl are hatched in a downy plumage that completely covers the body and makes it possible for the bird to go into the water shortly after hatching. This down, although relatively soft, differs considerably from the adult's down in that there is a distinct feather shaft with noninterlocking barbs. The downy plumage is retained for a period of from about two weeks in small ducks to six weeks in the large swans.

One of the early obvious changes in feathering of young waterfowl is the appearance of the first tail feathers, which push out and replace the downy feathers attached to their tips. In the Magpie Goose this occurs during the week after hatching, but in all other waterfowl it is more delayed, and often the beginning of juvenal feathering around the shoulder region is visible before the tail feathers reach a length apparent in the field.

JUVENAL PLUMAGE

The pattern of feather development from the downy to the juvenal plumage is quite constant in waterfowl. As soon as this feathering becomes apparent in the shoulder region, it shortly appears also on the breast and rapidly extends down the belly as well as back from the shoulders. Head feathers then begin to appear, usually in a patchy fashion, until gradually juvenal feathers in the head area meet the feathered breast. As the downy tips break off from the body feathers, the bird begins to assume more and more of a uniform appearance, and the last area to remain conspicuously downy is the lower back in front of the tail. Development of the flight feathers and wing coverts is delayed until the rest of the body is well feathered. The pinions then grow almost simultaneously, with the inner ones sometimes slightly ahead of the outer ones. The flight feathers are fully grown by a minimum of five weeks in some ducks and small geese, to seventeen weeks in the largest swans. In Table 4 some fledging periods (periods between hatching and flight) are listed for species representing the various major groups of waterfowl, based on personal observations and published sources:

TABLE 4

FLEDGING PERIODS OF VARIOUS WATERFOWL

Species	Days
Magpie Goose	82
Fulvous Whistling Duck	55–63
Mute and Trumpeter Swans	100–120
Black and Bewick's Swans	105
Pink-footed Goose	58
Graylag Goose	53–57
Snow Goose	38–49
Hawaiian Goose	70–84
Canada Goose (large races)	63–86
Cackling Canada Goose	42
Ross' Goose	42
Freckled Duck	58–80
Shelducks	49–56
Egyptian Goose	88
Gadwall	49–63
Mallard	49–60
Northern Shoveler	39–60
Pintail	38–52
Blue-winged Teal	35–44
Redhead	56–73
Canvasback	54–68
European Pochard	49–56
Ring-necked Duck	49–56
White-winged Scoter	63–77
Common Goldeneye	56–62
Ruddy Duck	49–66

FIGURE 12. Plumage sequences of the Magpie Goose and Common Goldeneye. Left side, from top: Downy, juvenal (six weeks), immature (six months), and adult Magpie Goose (male). Right side: Downy, juvenal, immature (one year), breeding (or nuptial), and nonbreeding ("eclipse") plumages of male Common Goldeneye.

It is interesting to note that the arctic-breeding Cackling Canada Goose and Ross' Goose have fledging periods as short as some of the smaller ducks, whereas the more tropical Fulvous Whistling Duck has a leisurely two-month fledging period.

Waterfowl fledge in their juvenal plumage, and such juvenile birds can be recognized easily by their tail feathers, which have notched tips where the original downy ends have broken off. The juvenal plumage is retained in the true geese and swans for much of the first year of life, and yearling swans tend to be more grayish or brownish than adults, whereas juvenile geese often have distinctive upper wing covert patterns. The body plumage of such birds is at least partially molted during the spring following hatching, although the flight feathers are not replaced until summer.

The aberrant Magpie Goose molts from a grayish juvenal plumage into a more contrasting black and white immature plumage when it is only about six months old (Figure 12). Furthermore, the Magpie Goose has the unusual feature of molting its flight feathers during the seventh and eighth months of life (at least in captivity), but these feathers are replaced sequentially, so that the power of flight is never lost. Thus, corresponding primary feathers on each wing are molted simultaneously, starting at the innermost and proceeding outward. The secondary feathers are also molted at this same time, likewise in outward sequence. Judging from unverified observations of captive birds, it appears possible that the Ruddy-headed Goose and perhaps also the Andean and Kelp Geese likewise have a gradual wing molt.

NUPTIAL PLUMAGE

The true ducks scarcely attain their juvenal plumage before they begin to lose most of these newly acquired feathers and assume either a nonbreeding (immature) plumage or directly assume their breeding plumage. Except possibly for Ruddy Ducks, this postjuvenal molt involves only the body feathers and among different species appears to be rather variable in time and extent of molt. Thus, Ruddy Ducks and Black-headed Ducks have a well-developed, first-year nonbreeding plumage that is practically or entirely lacking in dabblers. In most dabbling ducks the prenuptial molt into the breeding plumage is completed by the time the birds are six months old, when they then are practically identical to the adults. Sea ducks such as goldeneyes, which do not breed their first year, molt from the juvenal plumage into an immature nonbreeding (or "basic") plumage, and not before the following fall is the first nuptial (or "alternate") plumage attained. Thereafter the nuptial plumage of males alternates semiannually with an eclipse plumage (Figure 12) similar to that of females.

By the end of their first year of life, all waterfowl will have lost the last remnants of their juvenal plumage; that is, their flight feathers and other wing feathers. In the case of immature swans and geese, the loss of these feathers often occurs before the breeding adults have molted, but in this there is likely to be considerable variation. In geese and swans the first indication of molt is the loss of some of the longer scapular feathers of the back. Then, within a few days, the flight feathers begin to fall out (Plate 15). This loss may occur very rapidly if the bird is forced into strenuous exercise, or may be prolonged over several days, with the inner tertials and secondaries tending to fall before the primaries. The tail feathers are also molted at approximately this time, normally from the center outward, but usually not in an exact outward sequence.

Breeding geese and swans seem to have a more precise timing of their molt than do nonbreeding birds. Molt among breeding birds occurs typically shortly after the cygnets or goslings have hatched. Usually within two weeks after hatching has occurred the female begins her molt, normally followed several weeks later by that of the male. The flightless period of swans probably averages from six to eight weeks; of geese, about four to five weeks. The female is often almost ready to fly again by the time the male begins his wing molt, which in turn is normally completed about the time the young are fledged. By such a timing of molt one of the parents is always effectively able to defend the brood, and the whole family is ready to fly off together as soon as the young are finally fledged.

In most ducks other than the shelducks, only the female cares for the young. The male, who normally deserts the female early in her incubation period, soon begins to molt into his eclipse plumage. The bright feathers of the male are lost rapidly, but in a rather irregular sequence. In surface-feeding ducks the first feathers of the eclipse plumage usually appear on the flanks, scapulars (shoulders), and upper tail coverts, while the bright head colors are lost at the same time or shortly afterward. The tail begins to molt from the center outward at about the same time as the innermost wing feathers are dropped. The important flight feathers are not lost until the male is well into his eclipse plumage and is protectively colored. During the time the male is thus flightless, the female is usually still sitting on eggs or is brooding young, and has not yet undergone her molt. She normally does not lose her flight feathers until the young are able to fly. During her flightless period of three to four weeks she abandons her brood, which soon flock together with other immature birds as well as with adults that have already completed the wing molt.

It seems to be true that males of most true ducks undergo two molts of body plumage, and one of wings, each year. In some groups, such as the dabbling ducks, the tail feathers may also be replaced twice each year, but in others, including the pochards and sea ducks, they evidently are molted only once. This double body molt of ducks is apparent among the species in which there are distinctly different nuptial and eclipse male plumages, but it is not so obvious in females or in species like the American Black Duck. Yet this species, together with probably many other dull-colored ducks, does have two body molts each year, although seasonal changes of appearance are barely evident. Molting of female waterfowl is obvious only among some shelducks and such species as Greater Scaup and Tufted Duck, in which the head pattern varies seasonally.

A double molt of the down feathers also occurs in females of at least some duck species, with longer and often darker down feathers being grown during early spring, at the same time the female molts into her nesting plumage. Milton Weller has found evidence that this incomplete spring molt of the female corresponds to the male's earlier prenuptial molt into its breeding plumage, rather than to the male's postnuptial molt, which may be occurring at about the same time or somewhat later.

ECLIPSE PLUMAGE

The occurrence of the eclipse plumage in males of many species of ducks has caused much speculation and confusion, for perhaps in no other group of birds is a definite nonbreeding plumage held for so short a period. Mallards are in breeding plumage for nine months and in nonbreeding or eclipse plumage for only three. However, in some species, such as the Garganey, the males are in breeding plumage for less than half the year. The North American race of the Ruddy Duck has a rather equal division of time between its breeding and non-breeding plumages. It seems clear, therefore, that the eclipse plumage is really nothing more than a variably compressed nonbreeding plumage. By shortening the period during which this dull plumage is worn, the birds have a longer period during which to display and form pairs. Species living in areas where the breeding season is very long, or where it is irregular and dependent upon rainfall, usually lack eclipse plumages. For example, it has been reported that the West Indian population of the Ruddy Duck lacks an eclipse plumage, and it is possible that the northern South American races also lack such a plumage.

Tropical, brightly colored species that totally lack eclipse plumages include the Ringed Teal, Brazilian Teal, two of the three species of pygmy geese, and a few others. The tropical races of the Cinnamon Teal are reported to have much shorter eclipse plumages than the North American population. One South American temperate zone species, the Chiloé Wigeon, also lacks a definite eclipse plumage and is fairly brightly colored in both sexes, providing an exception to the general rule.

In most cases the nonbreeding or eclipse plumage of males closely resembles the female. But the Long-tailed Duck, or Oldsquaw, has a summer plumage that is distinctly different from both its winter plumage and that of the female. Some workers have reported that this species has a partial third plumage intercalated between the summer and winter plumages. It appears that molt in the Long-tailed Duck is a greatly prolonged affair, and that the birds are molting almost continuously from April to November. As a result there seems to be some overlap between the completion of the summer plumage (Plate 108) and the assumption of the winter plumage, which may be a reason for the controversy regarding the number of molts in this species. Male scoters also undergo body molt almost continuously, but do not have any marked seasonal alternations of plumage appearance.

Another group of birds in which the eclipse plumage of the adult male differs from the female is in the larger eiders. These birds assume a remarkably dark-colored male plumage during the summer, giving them a very distinctive appearance quite unlike the breeding plumage. In Common Eiders, however, there seem to be several classes of nonbreeders. First year males assume a plumage that is distinctly barred and similar to that of the female, second-year birds are more blackish with some barring, and older males have an almost entirely black eclipse plumage.

Molts in the shelducks and sheldgeese have been little studied but pose some interesting problems. It has been reported that the sheldgeese have only a single body molt each year, but most of the shelducks clearly have two distinct plumages, and thus two molts, each year. This double molt is most evident in the Paradise Shelduck. In this New Zealand species the female, rather than the male, alternates between a dull nonbreeding (gray) and a brighter breeding (red) body plumage, whereas the male remains in a dull grayish plumage the year around. In addition, immature birds of this species resemble the gray male rather than the female. It seems that this brighter female plumage—also present to a lesser degree in the Ruddy, Cape, and Australian Shelducks—is related to the fact that in shelducks the female does the overt courting, and so it is the male who, in effect, chooses his mate. This behavior seems to explain the partial turnabout of the male and female plumages. Young shelducks of these species resemble the dull-colored male—evidently as a protective coloration adaptation.

Sometimes female ducks that are very old, or that have through some disease developed nonfunctional ovaries, assume a malelike plumage. Such a change apparently comes about because the male plumage in ducks is the "neutral" one, and unless it is prevented from developing by, for example, the presence of female sex hormones, it will tend to appear. The mechanism by which male ducks temporarily assume femalelike eclipse plumages is still unknown, as are the factors controlling femalelike feather patterns in juveniles. It is interesting that the male-like females mentioned above also often exhibit male courtship display patterns, indicating that sexual behavior responses too are fundamentally regulated by hormone levels and proportions.

8

Evolution and Hybridization

$\mathcal{T}$*HERE* is no doubt that evolutionary change is continually in progress in all species of waterfowl, and that currently living forms are constantly adapting to their changing environment. It is not correct, however, to say that all waterfowl are necessarily undergoing species proliferation. Only in those species composed of separated populations sufficiently isolated to prevent a significant amount of interbreeding can genetic differences accumulate and so eventually provide the basis for two or more potentially new species. Should such populations that have had prolonged isolation once again come into contact before speciation has been completed—because of climatic changes, topographic changes, or man's influence—then interaction and possibly hybridization are likely to occur. It is possible to find different examples of isolated waterfowl populations exhibiting no evident geographic variation, populations that have subdivided into numerous well-marked geographic races, and populations in which secondary contact has either resulted in a variable amount of interbreeding or in which two distinct species have resulted.

It is important to consider the rates at which evolutionary adaptation can occur, the potentialities for geographic isolation in different groups, and the probabilities of interspecies hybridization. All these factors can be influenced by differences in life cycles, breeding biology, and behavior among the various waterfowl groups. In swans and geese, for example, the life cycles are long, pair bonds relatively permanent, and sexual maturity is usually not reached before the third year. Clutch sizes are relatively small (typically from four to six eggs) and, if the first clutch is unsuccessful, renesting is unlikely. Therefore, although parental care by both sexes keeps egg and young mortality minimal, the chances of hatching a cygnet or gosling with a favorable mutation are small to begin with, and it may be three years before this mutation can start to spread into the population. Because there is a tendency in geese and swans to return to their natal home for nesting, the rate of dispersal of new genetic combinations to other populations is very low. However, because of the resulting inbreeding, distinctive local populations can readily develop, even without major geographic barriers to prevent mixing of breeding populations. Thus, such diverse races as the miniature Cackling Canada Goose and the "Giant" Canada Goose have evolved, which in a practical sense are almost two distinct species. In Europe and Asia the same thing has happened to the Bean Goose, which has also formed many geographic races. Geese and swans, therefore, can be characterized as groups in which the rate of evolutionary adaptation is relatively slow, but subspeciation is easily achieved.

The situation among the ducks is altogether different. In such groups as the dabbling ducks, which in number of species and population sizes are the most successful of all waterfowl, life cycles are short, pair bonds are renewed yearly, and sexual maturity is reached the first year. Clutch sizes are somewhat larger, often averaging eight eggs or more, and renesting after early nest loss is possible. Assuming that a favorable mutation occurs in a single case, within a year this bird potentially could produce eight or more offspring, which in turn could all reproduce before the hypothetical goose or swan mentioned above might have produced its first offspring. As shown in Figure 13, a Mallard's high average mortality rate is effectively counteracted by a rapid maturity and a greater cumulative reproductive potential, in contrast to a Canada Goose's lower mortality rate with a prolonged period of sexual immaturity and a lower reproductive potential. The resulting more rapid turnover rate in the Mallard's population makes it more vulnerable to yearly environmental variations, though it allows for more rapid changes in gene frequencies, whereas the Canada Goose has a greater inherent population stability and thus might not be so severely affected by a series of unfavorable breeding seasons. Although female ducks tend to return to their place of hatching when mature, males on the wintering grounds may mate with females that originated elsewhere, and thus a favorable mutation may soon spread across a continent. Such gene diffusion tends to inhibit continental subspeciation, but at the same time it keeps each species closely adapted to changing environments, and if a new mutation allows for better habitat exploitation, that adaptation can be spread rapidly. No doubt by these means such specialized forms as the Pink-eared Duck, Blue Duck, and many other "aberrant" species evolved.

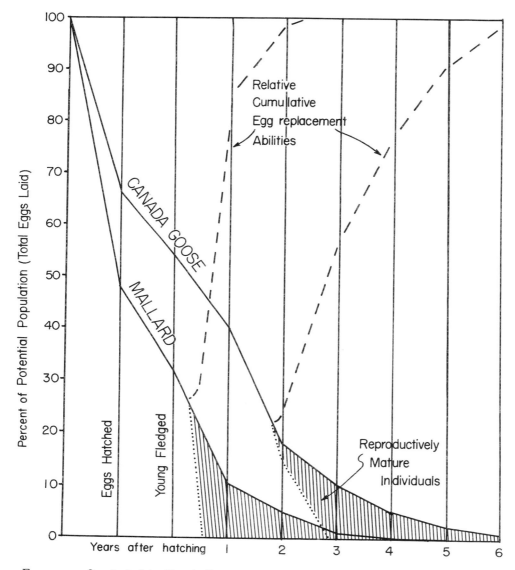

FIGURE 13. Survival of the Canada Goose and Mallard, based on banding data and field studies, showing the relative average mortality rates and expected relative egg-replacement abilities of the two species under natural conditions.

Rapidity of evolutionary adaptation in the form of anatomical and structural changes is not the only advantage ducks possess over geese. Because they have the genetic potentialities of readily modifying innate behavioral responses associated with pair formation, it is possible for "isolating mechanisms" preventing hybridization to be rapidly evolved, which means that two closely related species are able to occupy very similar ecological habitats without interbreeding. Such potentiality is reduced in geese and swans, in which courtship behavior patterns appear to be more rigidly maintained. Closely related geese and swans might thus be expected to hybridize if they breed in the same area, especially if they are of nearly the same body size and plumage pattern. However, closely related species of swans and geese usually differ in the colors and patterns of the head and bill region, and also generally have distinctly different vocalizations, both of which appear to be important in preventing hybridization.

Adaptations in courtship displays, plumage and soft part modifications, as well as vocalizations are probably primarily responsible among ducks for the prevention of hybridization. The reasons for advancing this idea are numerous. A listing of the species of ducks having the widest ranges and consequently having contact with the largest number of related species shows that such species inevitably have elaborate male plumages and displays. Examples include the Common Mallard, Northern Pintail, Northern Green-winged Teal, and Northern Shoveler. However, when these species are "marooned" on oceanic islands, or otherwise separated from all other species, the bright male plumages are quickly lost. Such plumage changes occurred, for example, in the Hawaiian and Laysan Island races of Mallard, the Fanning Islands race of the Gadwall, the Kerguelen and Crozet races of the Pintail, and the Galapagos race of the Bahama Pintail. This indicates that the main importance of the male plumage is not merely to stimulate females, but rather to help prevent females from accepting a mate of the wrong species. In the few instances of species lacking close relatives but having elaborate male plumages, such as the Ringed Teal, Torrent Duck, Harlequin Duck, and Long-tailed Duck, probably the primary reason for the evolution and maintenance of these features is "sexual selection," or the tendency of females to accept conspecific mates on the basis of their plumage and display characteristics.

SECONDARY CONTACT

When two populations from the same parental stock secondarily come together once again after prolonged isolation, what are the various possibilities that might result? There are several, although they tend to merge with one another. The first is that the two forms will not have diverged enough genetically to develop important ecological or behavioral differences, and thus individuals from the two stocks will interbreed. If the resulting progeny are fertile and well adapted to the environment, they will continue to interbreed among themselves and with both parental stocks; and eventually the two populations will amalgamate into one having the "best," or most adaptive, features of both. Something like this might have happened on the Mariana Islands (Guam, Saipan, and Tinian), where stock of the Mallard and "Gray Duck" (race of Spot-billed Duck) formed a "hybrid swarm" exhibiting features of both parental stocks. The same is also probably occurring in New Zealand and Australia where the introduced Mallard is currently hybridizing with the indigenous Mallardlike ducks.

If, at the time of secondary contact, sufficient genetic differences have developed in the two populations so that they do not interbreed at all, then they must be considered two species. Any ecological differences already existing between them are likely to be increased with time, reducing competition between the species.

There is also a third possibility, in the case of those populations that hybridize only infrequently when they achieve secondary contact. The resulting hybrids, because they have reduced fertility, intermediate plumages, and atypical display characteristics, or are poorly adapted to the environment may reproduce only poorly or not at all. This means that those birds from both populations having a tendency to hybridize will be "selected against," and those least prone to hybridize will have a more favorable chance of producing progeny. In this way the individual members of each population having traits which are most widely different from those of the other population will be favored, and the two populations will tend to diverge more rapidly than if they had not come into contact at all.

FREQUENCY OF HYBRIDIZATION

In spite of several built-in safeguards against hybridization in the form of plumage and behavioral differences, hybridization in waterfowl is relatively frequent. In fact, it may be asserted that waterfowl, perhaps more than any other avian family, are capable of an extreme genetic capacity for hybridization. Over four hundred kinds of interspecies hybrids have been reported for the waterfowl family alone. Most of these have occurred in captivity, but a surprising number have also been reported from the wild. Hybrids have been reported for most of the major groups except that of the Magpie Goose, which of course contains only a single species. The Freckled Duck and steamer ducks likewise are not known to have been hybridized. Of the other tribes, all but the whistling ducks and stiff-tails are believed to have been hybridized with members of other tribes. For example, the Mallard has hybridized in captivity with such diverse species as the Graylag Goose and the Goosander. Other equally unlikely captive-bred combinations include the Northern Shelduck's hybridization with the Goosander, and the Chestnut Teal's hybridization with the Long-tailed Duck. The record holders for hybridization are the Common Mallard, hybridized with approximately forty other species, and the North American Wood Duck, hybridized with over twenty species.

Wild-shot hybrids have sometimes been the source of much confusion. The so-called "Brewer's" or "Bimaculated" Duck, for example, which was named and painted by Audubon, proved to be a hybrid between the Common Mallard and Gadwall. The "Paget's Pochard" of Europe is a rather frequent hybrid combination between the European Pochard and Ferruginous White-eye; the "Oustalet's Duck" is the previously mentioned hybrid population of Mallards and Spot-billed Ducks of the Mariana Islands.

In North America the most frequent naturally hybridizing ducks are the Common Mallard and American Black Duck in the eastern states, and the Common Mallard and Mexican Duck in New Mexico. In combinations of such birds, where the male sex of one parental form has a metallic-colored head and the other parental species is dull-colored, the resulting male hybrids often have metallic coloration around and behind the eyes, but the rest of the head is dull-colored. Otherwise, the plumage patterns are usually a "blend" of the two parental types, but there are often new and unusual patterns that also emerge in hybrids and that sometimes are reminiscent of other species. These may be the result of new gene combinations or possibly may represent the reappearance of ancestral plumage traits normally repressed in pure individuals. Examples include a "bridled" facial pattern similar to that of the Baikal Teal, which is found in many dabbling duck hybrids, and the facial crescent similar to that of the Blue-winged Teal, which often appears in shoveler hybrids.

The study of hybrids is one of the most instructive means of judging evolutionary relationships among species and, in addition, genetic studies of plumage or behavioral variations may be possible among fertile hybrid combinations. For example, it has been possible to study the inheritance of both male plumage characteristics and male display characteristics between the Common Mallard and the Northern Pintail, by controlled experiments in which first- and second-generation hybrids between these species were obtained. First-generation males exhibited a common blending of Mallard and Pintail plumage and display characteristics; but when second-generation hybrids were produced, a wide range of variants resulted, including a few very Pintaillike and Mallardlike birds (Plate 75). Interestingly, the Mallardlike males performed displays that closely approximated the Mallard ancestor, and the same was true of the particularly Pintaillike males. These results suggest that there is a common inheritance of plumage and behavioral traits in these species and that there is a relatively simple genetic control of both of these sets of characteristics related to courtship and formation of pairs.

↑ 117. Red-billed Pintail (adults)   ↓ 118. Silver Teal (adults)

↑ 119. Hottentot Teal (male calling)   ↓ 120. Garganey (pair, male on left)

↑ 121. Blue-winged Teal (pair)   ↓ 122. Cinnamon Teal (male tail-shaking)

↑ 123. Red Shoveler (pair, male on left)   ↓ 124. Cape Shoveler (pair, female in front)

↑ 125. Australasian Shoveler (male)　　　　↓ 126. Northern Shoveler (pair)

↑ 127. Cape Shoveler (male)   ↓ 128. Southern Pochard (male)

↑ 129. Rosy-billed Pochard   ↓ 130. Canvasback (pair, male calling)

↑ 131. European Pochard (pair)   ↓ 132. Ring-necked Duck (pair)

↑ 133. Australian White-eye (pair) ↓ 134. Baer's Pochard

↑ 135. Ferruginous White-eye   ↓ 136. New Zealand Scaup (pair)

↑ 137. Lesser Scaup [RICHARD MOSS] ↓ 138. Harlequin Duck [SVEN-AXEL BENGTSON]

↑ 139. Surf Scoter (female)   ↓ 140. White-winged Scoter (female)

↑ 141. Bufflehead (males)   ↓ 142. Common Goldeneye and Barrow's Goldeneye

↑ 143. Smew (male)   ↓ 144. Red-breasted Merganser (female)

↑ 145. Masked Duck family [D. HAGEMEYER]   ↓ 146. Argentine Ruddy Duck (males)

↑ 147. Maccoa Duck (female) [JOHN BEER]   ↓ 148. Australian Blue-billed Duck (male)

Some Unanswered Questions

9

LIKE all animal groups, the waterfowl have provided their share of questions or problems for biologists. Many of these have long since been resolved, but some remain. A few examples revolve around the identity of birds described in the past as new species, never to be found again, or to be later identified as hybrid individuals. Thus, Audubon's "Brewer's Duck" was relegated to the list of invalid species. One reverse situation, in which a bird first described as a hybrid was later found to be a new and distinct species, has also occurred. In 1890, the English ornithologist W. Sclater described a female duck shot near Vladivostok, Siberia, as a probable hybrid between the Ruddy Shelduck and Falcated Duck. About thirty years later, the Japanese waterfowl authority, N. Kuroda, obtained a similar bird shot in 1916 and described it as a new species of shelduck. Finally, a male that had been shot in Korea in 1913 or 1914 was obtained by Kuroda in 1924, and the proof of the species was finally at hand. A most interesting fact about this species, called the Crested or Korean Shelduck (Figure 14), is that it was well known to early Japanese, who had named it and illustrated it in ancient manuscripts. Unfortunately, it appears that the bird became extinct just about the time that modern science finally recognized its existence, and no more specimens have been obtained, although a few persons have reported possible sightings of this species.

Several other species of waterfowl have become extinct or are nearly extinct

77

FIGURE 14. Extinct species and subspecies of waterfowl. Upper left: Crested Shelduck (male). Upper right: Labrador Duck (male). Middle left: Pink-headed Duck (male). Middle right: Auckland Island Merganser (sexes alike). Lower left: "Coues' Gadwall" (race of Gadwall). Lower right: Bering race of Canada Goose (sexes alike).

from unknown causes. The best known case is that of the Labrador Duck, a small sea duck that apparently was fairly common along the eastern coast of the United States in the early 1800's (Figure 14). Although specimens were sold on the New York market as late as 1860, nothing was known of the species' biology or its nesting areas, presumed to have been in Labrador. The species evidently became extinct so rapidly that little or no attempt was made to preserve specimens. Thus, not a single complete skeleton is present in any museum, and only about sixty skins and mounted specimens are known to exist.

STRUGGLE FOR SURVIVAL

A few uncertainties have existed regarding the survival or possible extinction of some of the races of the Canada Goose. Of the twelve described subspecies of this species, at least two were regarded until recently as apparently extinct. A small race of this goose bred on the Commander and Kurile Islands, in the Bering Sea, until about 1900. This bird, the Bering Canada Goose, was about the size of the Cackling Canada Goose, but has a large white ring at the base of the black neck (Figure 14). Evidently it is now extinct, probably because of predator introduction and other human activities on these islands. A very similar goose, the Aleutian Canada Goose, is a slightly larger bird also tending to have white at the base of the neck. This race once bred on the many islands of the Aleutian chain, wintering in Japan and along the western coast of North America. The bird was probably never very abundant, but man's introduction of predatory mammals gradually ruined most of the islands for breeding. In recent years no breeding populations were known, but in 1962 several families were found on Buldir Island, the most remote and isolated of all the Aleutian Islands. In 1963 several broods of goslings were caught and brought into captivity in hopes of eventually establishing other breeding populations.

One of the waterfowl "myths" that proved to be a fact was a giant race of the Canada Goose to which hunters in the Dakotas frequently referred and occasionally shot in the early 1900's. These birds apparently once bred over much of the Great Plains before agriculture destroyed the original prairies, and by the 1940's it was assumed that these immense geese, weighing up to fourteen or eighteen pounds, must have gone the way of the Passenger Pigeon. Surprisingly, however, a flock of geese that have wintered yearly at Rochester, Minnesota, were recently found in 1962 to be in this size range. These birds have since been traced to their nesting grounds in central Manitoba, and several additional flocks have also been located, so that the race is not now regarded as in any real danger of extinction.

A duck that probably is now extinct, from unknown causes, is the Auckland Islands Merganser, found only on those small islands off the south coast of New Zealand (Figure 14). The species was discovered in 1840 and was apparently rare even at that time; it was last observed in 1909. Man cannot be blamed directly for the disappearance of this bird, for the islands were never colonized or markedly affected by human activities. Probably the early population of the species was always small, and thus in serious danger of extinction. This also is the presumed cause of the extinction of the "Coues' Gadwall," a race of the Gadwall that occurred on one or two small islands of the southwest Pacific, in the Fanning group (Figure 14). It was first found and a pair collected in 1874, but it has never been seen again. Like most island forms, it was smaller and the males were duller than the continental form.

The unique Pink-headed Duck provides a last example of a bird that recently lost its struggle for survival and now can only be written off as "probably extinct." Like the Labrador Duck, there was apparently a rapid demise of this species that was not appreciated by humans until it was too late. Salim Ali has summarized our meager knowledge about this bird, which was limited to northern India. Although never common, the male, with its unbelievably bright "blushing" pink head, was a beautiful bird that was first described in 1790 (Figure 14). A few nests were found, but the young were never described. Several pairs were kept in captivity in India and England during the early 1900's. The last reliable sight record was obtained in 1935, and most authorities believe that sufficient searches have been made to be certain that no more birds exist alive. Unfortunately, the birds placed in captivity never bred, nor were they studied sufficiently to provide any detailed information on molt or behavior. It has only recently become apparent that, on the basis of its tracheal anatomy, the Pink-headed Duck was probably more closely related to the pochards than to the dabbling ducks, with which it has generally been grouped.

The type of uncertainty just mentioned, of doubts as to a species' nearest "blood relatives," provides the kind of puzzle that appeals to every taxonomist. He plays the role of the biological detective, ferreting out every bit of available information about anatomy, behavior, fossil record, and so forth, in an effort to solve the complex problems of evolutionary relationships. In a family the size of the Anatidae, with nearly 150 living species, the range of such problems is practically indeterminate, but the problems vary greatly in their complexity. In fact, it is probably true that the major problems of waterfowl relationships have been worked out to the satisfaction of most biologists, although a good deal of quarreling might go on about such details as the most appropriate spelling of scientific names or optimum degree of generic "lumping." This statement may be true for over 90 per cent of the waterfowl species, but the remaining 10 per cent provide some of the most challenging problems, and a few of these still remain to be satisfactorily solved. Four examples will be mentioned here.

One of the minor problems puzzling ornithologists centers on the relationships of the drab-colored Marbled Teal. Different authorities have suggested that it might be most closely related to one or another of the typical dabbling ducks, such as the Mallard, Blue-winged Teal, Pintail, Gadwall, and, most recently, the Cape Teal. There seemed little question that it belonged in the vast genus *Anas* along with these other dabbling ducks, but somehow it did not fit neatly anywhere. Such features as the nonmetallic speculum and the fact that hybridization had been recorded only with the Ferruginous White-eye (a pochard) did little to ease the problem, and it was only when a study of its behavior was undertaken that the pieces began to fall together. It was discovered that in its sexual behavior, the Marbled Teal has more in common with the pochards than with the dabbling ducks. Later this evidence gained support when the male's trachea was found to have membranaceous "windows," exactly as those that occur in the pochards but that are never found in the true dabbling ducks.

Another species providing a sort of taxonomic conundrum is the Coscoroba Swan. This strange bird presents an assortment of features which, like the elephant to the blind men, can be differently interpreted by different people. There is no doubt that the bird is basically swanlike, but its honking voice and its head, which is feathered in front of the eyes, are reminiscent of geese. However, its bill is flattened and like those of the dabbling ducks. Finally, the downy young exhibit a slight similarity to those of whistling ducks. Recent authorities have suggested that it may represent either a link between the swans and true geese or between the swans and whistling ducks. Supporting the latter view is the fact that the Coscoroba Swan appears to be the only swan lacking a *Triumph Ceremony*.

The White-backed Duck of Africa and Madagascar is a species that seems specifically designed to confuse taxonomists. It is a small, dumpy duck with a completely undistinguished appearance. Although the species' scientific name means in Greek "sea bird with a white back," it is doubtful that White-backed Ducks ever normally come within sight of the sea, and the white back is visible only during the infrequent occasions when the bird takes flight. Instead, members of this species typically sit about on ponds diving for food, sleeping, and occasionally uttering plaintive whistles that might be easily attributed to a guinea pig. Although they have historically been considered relatives of the stiff-tailed ducks, there is little evidence favoring this view. Their tails are short, unstiffened, and never cocked; males lack blue bills and inflatable neck pouches, and they never perform the elaborate mating displays typical of the stiff-tails. Furthermore, the downy young do not remotely resemble stiff-tail ducklings, but rather are uniquely blotched with rufous and tawny, and have a faintly visible nape stripe. Recently it has been discovered that in the species' copulatory behavior as well as its general breeding biology and downy vocalizations, the White-backed Duck is clearly related to the whistling ducks. This view is supported by its tarsal surface configuration and other anatomical features as well.

One last taxonomic problem, and possibly the most perplexing, is provided by the Freckled Duck, which is the rarest and certainly the least known of Australian waterfowl. In 1964, I had an opportunity to study a flock of wild Freckled Ducks over an extended period, recording several unusual behavioral characteristics. These include the facts that the birds normally take flight by running over the water in the manner of diving ducks, geese, and swans; that they apparently lack elaborate pair-forming ceremonies; and that they possess a mutual neck-stretching display somewhat similar to the *Triumph Ceremony* of geese and swans. These points tend to support anatomical evidence that the Freckled Duck might be related to the swans and geese rather than to the typical ducks, a view which is also suggested by the Freckled Duck's swanlike downy plumage pattern.

10

Waterfowl, Man, and the Future

$\mathcal{M}_{AN}$ has exploited the waterfowl to a greater degree than most other groups of birds. The Anatidae have provided an almost unlimited source of meat, eggs, feathers, down, and sporting pleasure over many parts of the world. Two species of ducks and two species of geese have been thoroughly domesticated, and several others might be considered semidomesticated.

The Mallard is certainly the most important domesticated species of waterfowl, though several domestic forms such as the Rouen, Pekin, Indian Runner, and Aylesbury have proved to be valuable sources of food and eggs for many centuries. The question concerning who first domesticated Mallards is debatable; however, the Pekin, which presumably originated in ancient China, is thought by some to be the oldest variety.

The Muscovy Duck of Central and South America was apparently domesticated originally by the Incas of Peru before the discovery of America by the Europeans. It was taken to Europe during the 1500's where it was given the inappropriate English name of Muscovy. In America this species is not raised nearly so frequently as is the Mallard.

Among the geese, the Graylag has provided the most important domesticated offshoots. This species gave rise to the common barnyard goose, including such varieties as the Embden, Toulouse, and Sebastopol. Like all domesticated forms, these birds are heavier, more awkward, and vary greatly in color from the original wild type. The Graylag, which originally ranged through most of Europe, was domesticated in ancient times and is frequently mentioned in early Roman literature. A second species of goose, the Swan Goose, was apparently more recently domesticated. This domesticated bird, generally called the "Chinese Goose," is characterized by having a longer bill than the Graylag, and by having a forehead enlargement that is lacking in the wild type.

The Mute Swan, also of Europe and Asia, might be considered at least a semidomesticated bird through much of its present range. Feral populations derived from originally captive stock on the east coast of North America also have increased rapidly in recent years. Numerous legends and myths concern Mute Swans, which were kept by both the Romans and Greeks. The "Polish Swan" is a color variety of the Mute in which the downy young and immature birds are white rather than gray, and the adults have flesh-colored, rather than black, feet.

Lastly, the Egyptian Goose might be mentioned as a species that has been at least partially domesticated for centuries. It was considered a sacred bird by the Egyptians, often appearing in their art, and was also kept by the Greeks and Romans. These nervous and highly vocal birds are very sensitive to disturbance, having sometimes been used as "watchdogs." A few minor color variations have been produced in captivity, but the domestic "African Goose" is actually a variety of the Swan Goose.

Although not truly domesticated, the eiders have been exploited for their down in an interesting manner in several areas of the arctic where they breed. In the Common Eider this exploitation has developed into a major industry in such places as Iceland, where the down is collected for commercial use in sleeping bags and pillows. The female eiders nest in colonies and are protected from predation by the "down farmers," persons who watch over them and even provide nesting places. After the female completes a clutch, but before incubation begins, most of the down is taken from the nest. The female then plucks additional down and feathers from her breast to replenish the nest during incubation. Finally, after the eggs are hatched, the remaining down is collected by the farmers. Thus, two "crops" of down are obtained each season from every laying female, without resorting to killing her. This unusual example of mutualism between man and bird is all too rare in modern society. In fact, man's tendency to overexploit seemingly limitless resources has inevitably led to a nearly universal reduction in waterfowl populations and the utter destruction of some species. The sad tale of extinction has been told for several species already, and as many or more species exist in precariously small populations.

ENDANGERED SPECIES

Intelligent use of the opportunities provided by aviculture for saving disappearing species has been achieved in the case of the "Laysan Teal," a small and inbred race of the Mallard that is restricted to the only lake on that tiny mid-Pacific island. Rabbits, introduced in 1903, increased so rapidly that within twenty years they had destroyed almost all vegetation on the island. This threat, together with the occasional depredations of man, reduced the "Laysan Teal" population to possibly less than thirty in the early part of the twentieth century. For several decades it held on by this thin thread but, surprisingly, in the 1950's it began a comeback, so that at present more than six hundred birds are believed to be alive. Several have been captured and placed in various bird collections, where many additional individuals have been reared.

At least two southern hemisphere species, and possibly more, are dangerously close to extinction. One of these is the New Zealand Brown Teal, once generally distributed over that island but now restricted to only a few localities. Three races exist, of which two (on the Campbell and Auckland Islands) are almost flightless. No accurate population estimates are available, but probably the total population of all three races numbers only in the hundreds, and the Campbell Island form may already be extinct. Efforts are being made to breed the species in captivity, and some success has been achieved at the Wildfowl Trust. Another New Zealand species threatened by extinction is the stream-dwelling Blue Duck. Like the Brown Teal, ducks of this species have suffered greatly from introduced predators and habitat disturbance. Furthermore, they have a tame disposition that renders them susceptible to predators. In this way they differ from the South American Torrent Duck (Figure 15), which is highly wary and probably suffers mostly from habitat disturbance and pollution, especially in Colombia, where it is now quite rare. It is, however, still abundant in Chile and Argentina.

Most Americans are familiar with the story of the struggle to save the Trumpeter Swan from the almost certain extinction that faced it in the early 1930's, when less than one hundred birds were known to exist. Through strict protection and constant watchfulness, this number has been increased to the point where nearly two thousand of these fine birds are present. Many of them are to be found on the Red Rock Lakes refuge of southwestern Montana, near Yellowstone Park, but a separate breeding population has also been discovered in the Copper River basin of Alaska. In recent years small numbers have been moved to various other refuges in an attempt to encourage breeding elsewhere, and this has been achieved in several places such as LaCreek National Wildlife Refuge, in southern South Dakota.

FIGURE 15. Some rare or little studied species of waterfowl; males illustrated. Upper left: Chinese Merganser. Upper right: Brazilian Merganser. Middle left: Chilean race of Torrent Duck. Middle right: Masked Duck. Lower left: White-headed Duck. Lower right: Green Pygmy Goose.

Another species apparently rescued at the last possible moment is the Hawaiian Goose, or Nene. This terrestrial goose inhabited the rocky lava slopes of the Hawaiian Islands, and probably was never extremely abundant, perhaps numbering about twenty-five thousand in the 1800's. Man's activities, particularly the introduction of such mammalian predators as pigs and dogs, nearly spelled doom for this beautiful goose. The population low point was reached about 1950, when less than fifty birds were known to exist, including about thirty wild birds on the island of Hawaii. A male and two females were then obtained by the Wild-fowl Trust in a last-ditch attempt to save the species, from which several hundred birds have been produced. This effort represents what is perhaps the most successful example of the use of aviculture to save a species, and there is every hope that the present wild population of some two hundred birds on the island of Hawaii can be successfully supplemented through the release of birds reared in captivity. Already some birds have been released there and reintroduced on the island of Maui, and this latter flock now numbers over one hundred.

The Hawaiian race of the Mallard, the Hawaiian Duck or Koloa, is also in serious danger of extinction at present. Like most island forms, its population is intrinsically small, possibly numbering no more than three hundred birds, mainly occurring on the island of Kauai. Every attempt is being made by the government to protect and encourage natural reproduction in the species. So far, little success has been achieved in breeding these birds in captivity.

One of the rarest ducks of South America, the Brazilian Merganser, was for some time feared to be extinct, since no birds had been observed since 1922. But in 1948 it was rediscovered in the northeasternmost province of Argentina, between Paraguay and Uruguay, where it evidently is still present in considerable numbers (Figure 15). A related species, the Chinese Merganser, occurs in unknown but presumably adequate numbers in eastern Asia; unfortunately it has never been brought into captivity where it could be readily studied, nor has any significant amount of information on its breeding biology been obtained (Figure 15). These two species, like the Labrador Duck and the Crested Shelduck, could easily become extinct before biologists are able to learn anything more than the barest facts about their existence.

Closer to home, the United States population of the Mexican Duck, a dull-colored and sedentary race of the Mallard, is barely surviving in extremely small numbers in southern New Mexico. Including the much larger Mexican range, the total maximum population may number only about ten thousand birds, and probably is actually less. Although this might appear to be a comfortable figure, any duck species that is extensively hunted will have a large yearly population turnover, and it is quite possible that the combination of uncontrolled habitat destruction and relatively unregulated hunting that now prevail in Mexico will soon destroy this entire population in a few more years.

FIGURE 16. The Trumpeter Swan, the largest of all Anatidae and the rarest of North American waterfowl.

TOWARD THE FUTURE

The picture that has emerged from this rapid review of the relationship between man and waterfowl is not a pleasant one. During the past hundred years the Labrador Duck, the Auckland Island Merganser, the Pink-headed Duck, and the Crested Shelduck have apparently all been completely destroyed, and several more species are in critical situations. With the world's constantly increasing human population, and the resulting economic pressures to turn the remaining wild lands into croplands, one cannot look to the future with optimism. Only through continued efforts to educate the public regarding their moral responsibilities of sharing this world with other animals, to teach people that it is possible to derive as much or more pleasure from watching and studying wild animals as from shooting them, and to preserve natural areas for the preservation and propagation of endangered species, will it be possible to show our descendants the extraordinary beauty and incalculable value of waterfowl. Let us act so that the legacy provided by the sight of wild ducks slanting into a prairie marsh against a flame-red sunset, the vernal recrudescence of life expressed in a skein of migrating geese darkly projected against an April-blue sky, or the ethereal majesty of distant swans' voices softly penetrating the morning mists of October will not be relinquished willingly by our own generation or by those that inherit these riches from us.

11

Identification of
Unfamiliar Waterfowl

HE most efficient method of identifying an unknown species of waterfowl that can be closely observed is by a systematic narrowing down of the possible kinds that it might be. The most common method by which this is achieved is the use of a descriptive key, such as that given below, which should enable the reader to identify to their proper genera at least the adults of unfamiliar waterfowl that can be examined in the hand or at very close range. Apart from two extinct genera which are not included in the key, representative species of all the genera likely to be encountered by the average reader should be readily identifiable by careful use of the key.

The procedure, as in the use of all such keys, is to choose which of two alternative descriptive couplets (A or A′, a or a′, and following pairs of numbers) best fits the unknown bird. Having chosen one of these, the pair of descriptive couplets immediately below the chosen alternative is then considered, without further regard for possibilities listed below the rejected alternative. In this manner a single genus will ultimately be reached, and no more than ten such couplets will have to be considered to identify any of the forty-one extant genera included in the key. After one has determined the identity of the genus with reasonable certainty, descriptions of the species of that genus should be consulted in the subsequent annotated list of waterfowl species. All these genera have from one to no more than twelve species, except the large dabbling duck genus *Anas*, for which a key to smaller subgroups is also included. By the combination of indicated plumage criteria, weights or measurements, and geographic ranges, it should be possible to identify the bird readily, to the species in most cases. Illustrations in this book or in other references can then be compared with the bird in question. Since immature and nonbreeding plumages are not always sufficiently like the breeding plumages to fit the short and general descriptions given in the keys, identification of all unknown waterfowl cannot be promised. However, the key has been devised to take such plumages into account wherever possible. Illustrations of many of the confusing nonbreeding plumages of waterfowl may be found in Delacour's *Waterfowl of the World*, which also includes species identification keys for most genera.

KEY TO THE GENERA OF ANATIDAE, EXCLUSIVE OF EXTINCT FORMS

A. Legs with completely reticulated (networklike) scale pattern, sexes very similar in color and voice, lacking iridescent coloration
   a. Feet nearly webless, hind toe long, legs relatively long ... Subfamily Anseranatinae (Magpie Goose, *Anseranas semipalmata*, only living species)
   a'. Feet distinctly webbed, hind toe short, legs short or long ... Subfamily Anserinae
      1. Smaller (under 22″ long), ducklike birds
         2. Relatively long legs (feet extended beyond tail in flight), rounded wings, and with whistling voices ... Tribe Dendrocygnini (Whistling ducks)
            3. Varied in color, but never with white back feathers ... *Dendrocygna* (8 species)
            3. Tawny brown in color, except for a white back ... *Thalassornis* (1 species)
         2. Legs do not extend beyond tail, wings pointed, and adults lack pure whistles ... Tribe Stictonettini (Freckled Duck, *Stictonetta naevosa*, only living species)
      1. Larger (usually over 24″ long), relatively slim-necked birds ... Tribe Anserini (Swans and true geese)
         4. Lores (area between eyes and bill) bare, neck as long as body or longer ... *Cygnus* (5 species)
         4. Lores feathered, neck usually shorter than body
            5. Mostly white (black wing tips), bill flattened and ducklike ... *Coscoroba* (1 species)

5. Mostly gray to brown or black in color (two species primarily white), bill with serrated edges for grazing

    6. A conspicuous green enlargement present on bill . . . *Cereopsis* (1 species)

    6. Lacking a conspicuous green enlargement on bill

        7. Plumage usually grayish, brownish or white, without much black on head or neck, bills, legs and feet variously colored . . . *Anser* (9 species)

        7. Plumage dark, with black markings on neck or head; bill, legs, and feet all black . . . *Branta* (5 species)

A′. Legs with lower part of tarsus having scutellate (vertically aligned) scales in front, sexes often different in color and voice; iridescent coloration frequent on wings or body, especially among males . . . Subfamily Anatinae

  a. Feet having weakly lobed hind toe (except *Hymenolaimus*), iridescent coloration frequent on wings, primarily surface-feeding or grazing birds that can take off water directly without running . . . Tribes Tadornini, Cairinini, and Anatini (see other couplet a′ on page 95)

    1. Relatively large (usually over 24″ long), with bony knob at bend of wing, most species having white upper wing coverts and iridescent green wing speculum . . . Tribe Tadornini (Sheldgeese and shelducks)

    2. Upper wing coverts not white, either pale blue or blackish

        3. Wing coverts blackish, white present on inner secondaries . . . *Neochen* (1 species)

        3. Wing coverts pale blue, no white present on secondaries . . . *Cyanochen* (1 species)

    2. Upper wing coverts white

        4. Iridescent wing speculum formed by secondary coverts (but lacking in adult males of one species in which wings are completely white), the secondaries being white . . . *Chloephaga* (5 species)

        4. Speculum formed by the secondaries, and their anterior coverts are white

            5. Secondary coverts have a distinct black line bordering front of speculum, large birds 28–30″ long . . . *Alopochen* (1 species)

            5. Secondary coverts usually lacking black line (present in only one species), length under 28″ . . . *Tadorna* (6 living species)

    1. Size varied, but if upper wing coverts are white, then large (over 26″) and rest of wing is iridescent in color (Cairinini), or smaller (under 24″) and lacking bony knob on wing (*Anas*)

6. Toes with sharp claws for perching, tail usually fairly long and broad, iridescence on upper wing surface often extending to primaries and wing coverts, under wing surfaces often blackish . . . Tribe Cairinini (Perching ducks)

    7. Relatively large (over 26″), upper wing coverts partly white, metallic iridescence extensive over body, bare facial skin frequent

        8. Spur present on bend of wing, long-legged . . . *Plectropterus* (1 species)

        8. No spur on wing, short-legged . . . *Cairina* (2 species)

    7. Usually smaller (mostly under 24″), upper wing coverts never white, head entirely feathered

        9. Upper wing surface uniformly dark and with metallic iridescence, head speckled with black, length 22–30″ . . . *Sarkidiornis* (1 species)

        9. Upper wing surface usually with white markings present, at least not entirely iridescent; length under 24″

            10. Upper wing coverts bluish, body chestnut brown, bill slightly enlarged at base . . . *Pteronetta* (1 species)

            10. With none of the above characteristics, mostly under 20″ long

                11. Bill about twice as long as high, adapted for grazing or crushing

                    12. Size very small (under 14″), upper wing coverts iridescent green . . . *Nettapus* (3 species)

                    12. Size larger (19–22″), green iridescence limited to secondaries, while their coverts are gray . . . *Chenonetta* (1 species)

                11. Bill more elongated relative to height, adapted to filter feeding

                    13. Speculum green and white, no white on primaries; under 17″ long

                        14. Speculum with wide white posterior border, feet red . . . *Amazonetta* (1 species)

                        14. Speculum with oval white anterior patch, feet pink . . . *Callonetta* (1 species)

                    13. Speculum blue or purple, outer vanes of primaries silvery white; over 17″ long . . . *Aix* (2 species)

6. Toes lacking sharp claws for perching, tail varied but usually not long and broad, iridescent color almost never present on wing coverts . . . Tribe Anatini (Dabbling ducks), plus *Heteronetta* of Tribe Oxyurini

15. No distinctly delimited wing speculum or other iridescent coloring, secondaries almost uniformly gray or rufous brown, sexes usually alike in plumage

    16. Bill normal in shape, not shovellike or soft-tipped; under 16″ long

        17. Body pale gray, tail over 3″ long ... *Marmaronetta* (1 species)

        17. Body brownish, tail under 2″ long ... *Heteronetta* (1 species)

    16. Upper mandible with soft, overhanging flap near tip

        18. Smaller (15–16″), with dark gray and white vertically barred body ... *Malacorhynchus* (1 species)

        18. Larger (22″), with uniformly lead-gray body ... *Hymenolaimus* (1 species)

15. Distinct, usually iridescent (rarely black or black and white) speculum present, sexes often unlike in plumage

    19. Tail feathers all very long (5″) and stiffened, wing spurs present, feet reddish in color ... *Merganetta* (1 species)

    19. Tail feathers not uniformly long and stiff, wing spurs absent or weakly developed, but if present feet not reddish ... *Anas* (36 species, see following key on page 97)

a′. Feet having strongly lobed hind toe, iridescent coloration usually lacking on wings but white wing markings common; primarily diving birds that must run along water to take off ... Tribes Tachyerini, Aythyini, Mergini, and Oxyurini (see also *Hymenolaimus* of Anatini)

20. Very large (over 26″), generally grayish or brownish heavy-set ducks with short wings having white wing patches and relatively short upcurled tails ... Tribe Tachyerini (Steamer ducks, *Tachyeres* only genus, with 3 species)

20. Mostly smaller (usually under 26″) and not so heavy-set; if over 26″, then with long stiffened tails or extensive black and white patterning

    21. Tail neither elongated nor stiffened, feet placed near center of body, neck not thick and short

        22. Upper wing surface uniformly grayish or brownish above except for white or gray stripe extending from inner secondaries toward primaries in some species, tail relatively short ... Tribe Aythyini (Pochards)

        23. Bill fairly narrow and straight in profile (enlarged basally in one species), uniformly bluish or red in color, distinct white wing-stripe present ... *Netta* (3 species)

23. Bill broader and somewhat concave in profile, usually slate gray or blue with pale area near nail, distinct wing stripe sometimes lacking . . . *Aythya* (12 species)

22. Primaries dark brown or blackish, white limited to secondary feathers or the wing coverts; tail often fairly long . . . Tribe Mergini (Sea ducks)

24. Upper and lower wing surfaces and body mostly or entirely dark brown or black, bill enlarged basally, white lacking in plumage or limited to head (and secondaries of one species) . . . *Melanitta* (3 species)

24. Wings not uniformly dark above and below or, if so, the body distinctly barred or otherwise patterned with white, pale gray, or buff

25. White markings on upper wing surface lacking or limited to the innermost secondaries and a few small spots on the upper coverts, underwing feathers dark-colored, bill about 1″ long

26. Bill narrow, with yellow or gray nail, without fleshy edge; secondaries iridescent purple or purplish brown . . . *Histrionicus* (1 species)

26. Bill broad, with fleshy edge and distinct black nail; secondaries chestnut or grayish brown . . . *Clangula* (1 species)

25. White or pale buff markings on upper wing surface; if faint or lacking, then bill about 2″ long and underwing linings pale brownish or grayish white (females of *Somateria*)

27. Bill narrow and serrated, with hooklike tip . . . *Mergus* (6 species)

27. Bill not narrow and serrated, and lacking hooklike tip

28. Innermost secondaries (tertials) straight, tapering to a point, and black or dark brown; white markings usually extensive on the other secondaries and their coverts; underwing feathers dark gray . . . *Bucephala* (3 species)

28. Innermost secondaries rounded and curved outward, often white; the remaining secondaries not predominantly white; underwing feathers pale gray or white

29. Secondaries iridescent purple with white borders, tail pointed, bill under 2″ and with soft edges; length usually under 19″ ... *Polysticta* (1 species)

29. Secondaries not iridescent, tail rounded, bill over 2″ and feathered nearly to nostrils; length over 19″ ... *Somateria* (3 species)

21. Tail feathers long and stiff, feet placed far toward the rear ... Tribe Oxyurini (Stiff-tailed ducks)

30. Adults over 24″ long, with 24 spiny tail feathers, male with pendent lobe under bill, which is less than one half the length of the head ... *Biziura* (1 species)

30. Adults under 20″ long, with no more than 18 spiny tail feathers, bill nearly one half the length of head and lacks pendent lobe ... *Oxyura* (6 species)

KEY TO SUBGROUPS OF THE GENUS *ANAS*, BASED ON WING PATTERNS

A. Upper wing coverts white, pale gray, or bluish

  a. Upper wing coverts white, silvery gray or blue-gray ... Wigeons (3 species); Falcated Duck and Garganey males

  a′. Upper wing coverts pale blue

    1. Bill normally shaped ... Blue-winged Teal and Cinnamon Teal

    1. Bill shovel-shaped ... Shovelers (4 species)

A′. Upper wing coverts more brownish, similar to primaries in color

  a. Speculum white, with gray or black outwardly, lacking iridescence ... Gadwall

  a′. Speculum not black and white, usually iridescent

    1. Speculum with white or black-and-white borders in front and behind, the white borders sometimes very narrow and occasionally lacking

      2. Speculum with one or more outer (and innermost) feathers black, otherwise usually iridescent green ... Cape, Gray, Madagascan, and Chestnut Teals

    2. Speculum with outer secondaries also iridescent

      3. Black border immediately ahead of speculum which is green, blue, or purple ... African Black Duck, Mallardlike ducks (6 species)

      3. White border immediately ahead of green speculum ... Salvadori's Duck, Silver and Hottentot Teals, Garganey females

1. Speculum bordered with buff or brown in front, buff or white posterior border in most
    4. Outer secondaries not primarily black; usually iridescent
        5. Speculum bronze-colored or brownish, with narrow white border behind . . . Bronze-winged Duck, Crested Duck, Northern Pintail
        5. Speculum green or blackish green, with broad buff posterior border . . . South American and African pintails (3 species)
    4. Outer secondaries mostly black; speculum otherwise iridescent green . . . Baikal, Brown and Green-winged Teals (2 species), Falcated Duck females

12

Annotated List of the Anatidae of the World

IN the list that follows, only full species are individually considered, although some well-marked subspecies are mentioned. For further information on subspecies and details of ranges, see Delacour's *Wildfowl of the World*. The indicated lengths are adult tip-of-bill to end-of-tail measurements, and in a few cases are only approximate. The weights indicated are in general averages for adults of both sexes; otherwise, available weight ranges are given.

SUBFAMILY ANSERANATINAE

I. *Tribe Anseranatini* (Magpie Goose)

1. Magpie or Semipalmated Goose (*Anseranas semipalmata*). An Australian gooselike bird with black and white plumage, long legs, a sturdy bill, and slightly webbed feet. Males are larger and have a higher frontal knob than do females. Length 30–34″. Average weights: females $4\frac{1}{2}$ lbs., males $6\frac{1}{10}$ lbs. Figure 12. Plate 27.

SUBFAMILY ANSERINAE

II. *Tribe Dendrocygnini* (Whistling Ducks)

1. Spotted Whistling Duck (*Dendrocygna guttata*). An East Indian species that can be identified by the combination of spotted flanks and a spotted bill.

The similar Black-billed Whistling Duck is larger and has a uniformly black bill. Length 17–19″. Plate 28.

2. Plumed Whistling Duck (*Dendrocygna eytoni*). An Australian species easily identified by its long buffy flank plumes. Like the preceding species, it too has a spotted bill. Length 16–18″. Average weight (both sexes) $1\frac{3}{4}$ lbs. Plate 1.

3. Fulvous Whistling Duck (*Dendrocygna bicolor*). A locally common species that is distributed widely (see text), identified by its overall fulvous coloration. Easily confused with the next species, it has a uniformly brownish breast and a usual call of only two syllables. Length 18–21″. Weight $1\frac{1}{2}$ to $1\frac{3}{4}$ lbs. Figure 7. Plate 2.

4. Wandering Whistling Duck (*Dendrocygna arcuata*). An East Indian and Australian species that has a conspicuous line of buffy feathers above its fulvous flanks, brownish underparts that are spotted with black in the breast region, and wings that whistle loudly in flight. The typical call is of many syllables. Length 16–18″. Average weight (both sexes) $1\frac{1}{3}$ lbs. Plate 3.

5. Lesser Whistling Duck (*Dendrocygna javanica*). An East Indian and southern Asiatic species that is the smallest of the whistling ducks. It is easily identified by the combination of small size, yellow eye-ring, and chestnut-colored upper tail coverts. Length 15–16″. Weight 1 to $1\frac{1}{3}$ lbs. Plate 29.

6. White-faced Whistling Duck (*Dendrocygna viduata*). An African and South American species that may be recognized by its white face and throat, sharply set off by an otherwise black head. Its triple-noted whistle is also distinctive. Length 16–18″. Weight $1\frac{1}{3}$ lbs. Plate 26.

7. Black-billed or Cuban Whistling Duck (*Dendrocygna arborea*). A West Indian species that is the largest of the whistling ducks. Apart from its size, the extensively spotted brown plumage and black bill are diagnostic. Length 19–23″. Weight $2\frac{1}{2}$ lbs. Plate 4.

8. Red-billed or Black-bellied Whistling Duck (*Dendrocygna autumnalis*). A Central and South American species that is readily recognized by its bright red bill, black underparts, and white upper wing coloration when in flight. One of the most vocal whistling ducks, it has a melodious, multisyllabic call. Length 19–21″. Weight $1\frac{5}{8}$ lbs. Plate 30.

9. White-backed Duck (*Thalassornis leuconotus*). Although usually included with the stiff-tailed ducks, this species of east and south Africa and Madagascar is here regarded as an aberrant whistling duck. The sexes are alike, with tawny bodies, yellowish necks, mottled heads, and robust black-spotted bills. Both sexes utter clear whistling notes, and usually dive for food. Length 15–16″. Weight $1\frac{1}{2}$ to $1\frac{3}{4}$ lbs. Plate 31.

III. *Tribe Anserini* (Swans and True Geese)

1. Mute Swan (*Cygnus olor*). The common swan of Europe and Asia, feral flocks of which occur in some eastern parts of the United States. Commonly kept in captivity, both sexes have black frontal knobs and thicker, more gracefully curving necks than do the other entirely white swans. Length 50–61″. Weight 25–30 lbs. Plates 5, 6, 32.

2. Black Swan (*Cygnus atratus*). An Australian swan that is unique in being entirely black except for white wing tips and that has a bright red bill. Length 45–55″. Average weights: females $11\frac{1}{4}$ lbs., males $13\frac{4}{5}$ lbs. Plate 7.

3. Black-necked Swan (*Cygnus melanocoryphus*). A small swan of southern South America, with white plumage except for a black head and neck. Length 39–49″. Weight 10–12 lbs. Plate 33.

4. Whooper Swan and Trumpeter Swan (*Cygnus cygnus*). Found in western North America (Trumpeter) and Eurasia (Whooper), these are the largest of the northern white swans. The adult Whooper (16–$22\frac{1}{2}$ lbs.) has an extensive amount of yellow on the bill; the larger Trumpeter, considered by some to be a distinct species, has none. Length 60–72″. Average weights: (Trumpeter) females $22\frac{1}{2}$ lbs., males 28 lbs. Figure 16. Plates 8, 10.

5. Whistling Swan and Bewick's Swan (*Cygnus columbianus*). Found in North America (Whistling) and Eurasia (Bewick's), these arctic-breeding swans are markedly smaller than the preceding similar species. The adult Bewick's Swan (15–$17\frac{1}{2}$ lbs.) has almost as much yellow on the bill as the adult Whooper; the adult Whistling Swan has very little or, rarely, none. Length 48–58″. Average weights: (Whistling) females $13\frac{4}{5}$ lbs., males $15\frac{3}{4}$ lbs. Plates 9, 34.

6. Coscoroba Swan (*Coscoroba coscoroba*). A southern South American species that is easily recognized by its white plumage except for black wing tips and by its bright red, ducklike bill. Length 35–45″. Average weights: females 7 lbs., males $8\frac{1}{3}$ lbs. Plate 35.

7. Swan Goose (*Anser cygnoides*). An Asian species with a long, black bill and a dark brown stripe extending down the back of the neck. The domesticated form ("Chinese goose") usually has a much enlarged forehead knob. Length 32–37″. Weight 5–8 lbs. Plate 11.

8. Bean Goose (*Anser fabalis*). A Eurasian species of "gray goose" with a black and yellow spotted bill and yellow feet. The smaller (24–30″), short-billed Pink-footed Goose, with pink feet and bill markings, is often considered a distinct species. Length 28–35″. Weight (Bean Goose) $5\frac{1}{2}$ to $9\frac{2}{5}$ lbs. Plate 12.

9. White-fronted Goose (*Anser albifrons*). A "gray goose" widely distributed throughout the northern hemisphere, recognized by the white forehead patch and black belly spotting (only in adults), and lacking the yellow eye-ring

of the next species. The bill is uniformly yellow to pink, and the feet are yellow to orange. Length 26–34″. Average weights: females 5 lbs., males $5\frac{1}{4}$ lbs. Plate 14.

10. Lesser White-fronted Goose (*Anser erythropus*). A small version of the preceding species found in northern Eurasia, but with a bright yellow eye-ring and the white forehead extending higher over the eyes. Length 21–26″. Weight $3\frac{1}{3}$ to $4\frac{2}{3}$ lbs. Plate 36.

11. Graylag Goose (*Anser anser*). A Eurasian "gray goose" with a uniformly yellow to pink bill, with little or no white on the forehead, and lacking belly spotting. It is the ancestor of the most common domesticated goose. Length 30–35″. Average weights: females $6\frac{4}{5}$ lbs., males $7\frac{1}{2}$ lbs. Plate 13.

12. Bar-headed Goose (*Anser indicus*). A goose from central Asia that is unique in its pale gray body and (in adults) a white head with two black bands behind the eyes. Its voice is a low, nasal honk reminiscent of an old horn. Length 28–30″. Weight $4\frac{2}{5}$ lbs. Plate 15.

13. Snow Goose (*Anser caerulescens*). A North American and eastern Siberian goose with two color phases, the "Snow" (white with black wing tips) and "Blue" (mostly slate gray with a white head) types. Intermediates also occur. The blue phase is chiefly found in the midwestern states during migration and winter. Both phases have black "grinning patches" along the sides of the bill. Length 26–33″. Average weights: Lesser Snow and "Blue" $4\frac{3}{4}$ lbs., Greater Snow $6\frac{1}{2}$ lbs. Plates 16, 17.

14. Ross' Goose (*Anser rossi*). A western North American miniature version of the Snow Goose, but with a noticeably shorter bill that lacks the "grinning patches" and tends to be bluish at the base. Length 21 to 26″. Average weights: females $2\frac{3}{4}$ lbs., males 3 lbs. Plate 18.

15. Emperor Goose (*Anser canagicus*). An Alaskan and eastern Siberian goose with a unique gray, white, and black "scaled" pattern throughout, except for a white head and hindneck, which is usually stained with rust in the wild. The species winters in the arctic seas, and is rarely found south of Alaska. Length 26–30″. Average weights: females 6 lbs., males $6\frac{1}{5}$ lbs. Plate 37.

16. Hawaiian Goose or Nene (*Branta sandvicensis*). A Hawaiian species, somewhat similar to the Canada Goose, except for a buff-colored cheek patch and neck, the latter with vertical dark striations. Length 22–28″. Average weights: females $4\frac{1}{2}$lbs., males $4\frac{7}{8}$ lbs. Plate 39.

17. Canada Goose (*Branta canadensis*). A widespread North American goose with a black head and neck except for a white cheek and throat patch. Highly variable in size and degree of body darkness, including a "Giant" race and several very small races such as the "Cackling Goose" and "Richardson's

Goose." Length 22–43″. Average weights: 3½ lbs. ("Cackling Goose") to 10 lbs. ("Giant" race). Figure 14. Plate 19.

18. Barnacle Goose (*Branta leucopsis*). An arctic-breeding Eurasian goose, superficially similar to the Canada Goose, but with the black of the neck extending over the breast and the white cheek patch continuous around the forehead. Length 23–28″. Average weights: females 4 lbs., males 4⅗ lbs. Figure 7. Plate 20.

19. Brant Goose (*Branta bernicla*). A small arctic-breeding and maritime goose of the northern hemisphere that is entirely black from head to breast, except for a small, incomplete, neck-ring. Several races occur, varying in degree of body darkness. Length 22–26″. Average weights: females 3⅘ lbs., males 4½ lbs. Plate 21.

20. Red-breasted Goose (*Branta ruficollis*). A small central Asian goose that is unique in having a reddish brown breast and cheeks, marked off in white and black. The broad white stripe above the otherwise black flanks is conspicuous, as is the sharp, doglike, barking voice. Length 21–22″. Weight 3 to 3⅘ lbs. Plate 40.

21. Cape Barren Goose (*Cereopsis novae-hollandiae*). An aberrant southern Australian goose that is rather uniformly gray with a white crown and an enlarged pea-green bill. This rare species is mostly limited to the islands off Australia's south coast. Semiterrestrial in habits, it has reduced foot webbing. Length 30–39″. Average weights: females 8⅓ lbs., males 11⅔ lbs. Plate 38.

IV. *Tribe Stictonettini* (Freckled Duck)

1. Freckled Duck (*Stictonetta naevosa*). A southern Australian and Tasmanian duck now believed to be related to the geese and swans, but usually included with the dabbling ducks. Both sexes are generally "oatmeal" brown and lack bright coloration. The darker head is slightly crested and the base of the male's bill becomes a brilliant red during the breeding season. Length 20–22″. Average weights: females 1⅗ lbs., males 2⅓ lbs. Plate 41.

V. *Tribe Tadornini* (Sheldgeese and Shelducks)

1. Blue-winged Goose (*Cyanochen cyanopterus*). A sheldgoose from the highlands of Abyssinia (Ethiopia); both sexes are grayish except for pale blue upperwing coverts and a green speculum. Individuals characteristically walk or swim with the head resting on the back. Length 23–29″. Plate 42.

2. Andean Goose (*Chloephaga melanoptera*). A large western South American species of sheldgoose, in which both sexes are mostly white but with black wing tips and tail, and a spotted black and white back. Length 29–32″. Weight 6–8 lbs. Plate 22.

3. Magellan or Upland Goose (*Chloephaga picta*). A southern South American and Falkland Island species of sheldgoose. The male has a white head and variably barred black and white flanks; the female has a chocolate brown head and heavily barred flanks. The Falkland Island race is larger and has pure white underparts, whereas these are often barred on the mainland form. Length 23–26″. Weight 6 lbs. (females) to 6¼ lbs. (males). Plate 43.

4. Kelp Goose (*Chloephaga hybrida*). A southern South American maritime sheldgoose with extreme sexual dimorphism: the adult male is pure white with a black bill and yellow legs; the female is a heavily barred, dark brown bird, with white hindquarters and wing coverts. Length 22–25″. Weight 5 lbs. Plate 23.

5. Ashy-headed Goose (*Chloephaga poliocephala*). A relatively small southern South American sheldgoose in which the sexes are alike, with grayish heads, white eye-rings, reddish-brown breasts, and black and white barred flanks. Length 20–22″. Plate 24.

6. Ruddy-headed Goose (*Chloephaga rubidiceps*). A very small southern South American sheldgoose. The sexes are alike, with brownish heads, white eye-rings, and dark bodies barred with rufous, gray, and black. Length 18–20″. Weight 4½ lbs. Plate 25.

7. Orinoco Goose (*Neochen jubatus*). A South American forest-dwelling sheldgoose. The sexes are alike, with long red legs and buff-colored heads, necks, and breasts. The neck feathers are lengthened, producing a thick-necked effect. Unlike *Chloephaga*, it perches frequently. Length 24–26″. Plate 44.

8. Egyptian Goose (*Alopochen aegyptiacus*). An African sheldgoose in which the sexes are alike, with grayish bodies and brown patches on the abdomen and around the eyes. One of the most aggressive of the sheldgeese. Length 28–29″. Weight 4–6 lbs. Plate 45.

9. Ruddy Shelduck (*Tadorna ferruginea*). A south Eurasian and north African shelduck that is rather uniformly rust-colored except for a white area around the eyes on females and a small black neck-ring on males. Length 25–26″. Average weights: females 2¾ lbs., males 3¾ lbs. Plate 53.

10. Cape Shelduck (*Tadorna cana*). A South African shelduck similar to the preceding species except for a gray head. Females also have a large white patch around the eyes. Length 25″. Plate 46.

11. Paradise Shelduck (*Tadorna variegata*). A New Zealand shelduck that exhibits great sexual variation in size and appearance: the female has a gray to reddish body and a pure white head, but the larger male has a dark gray body and an iridescent greenish-black head. Length 25–28″. Weight (females) 2⅘ lbs. Plate 54.

12. Crested or Korean Shelduck (*Tadorna cristata*). An apparently extinct species from Korea and southeastern Siberia. Both sexes possessed a black crest;

otherwise, the head was mostly white in females and gray in males. Length 25″ (estimated). Figure 14.

13. Australian Shelduck (*Tadorna tadornoides*). A southern Australian and Tasmanian species in which the sexes are similar, with dark green heads, white neck-rings, and brown breasts. The female has a small white eye-patch. Length 25–28″. Average weights: females 2⅘ lbs., males 3⅔ lbs. Plate 55.

14. Northern or Common Shelduck (*Tadorna tadorna*). A Eurasian species that is generally white except for a green head, a broad brown breast band, and black on the wings. The sexes are nearly alike except for a large red frontal knob on the bill of the male. Length 24″. Weight 2½ to 3½ lbs. Figure 7. Plate 56.

15. Radjah Shelduck (*Tadorna radjah*). A northern Australian and East Indian species, the only shelduck that has pure white plumage on the head, breast, and flanks, interrupted only by a narrow brown breast band. The sexes are identical in appearance, but the male has a wheezy, whistling call. Length 20–24″. Average weights: females 1⅘ lbs., males 2 lbs. Plate 47.

VI. *Tribe Tachyerini* (Steamer Ducks)

1. Flying Steamer Duck (*Tachyeres patachonicus*). A species of southern South America and of the Falkland Islands. Like all steamer ducks, this species somewhat resembles a large domestic Mallard, except that it has generally reddish gray coloration apart from a white speculum. This species is darker and smaller than the two following ones; the females have browner heads with narrow white eye-stripes, whereas males have gray heads with brownish throats. Length 26–28″. Average weights: females 5¾ lbs., males 6⅘ lbs. Figure 7.

2. Magellanic Flightless Steamer Duck (*Tachyeres pteneres*). A southern South American species, the largest and grayest of the three species of steamer ducks. Both sexes are incapable of flight, have a small amount of brownish coloration on the throat, and are otherwise gray. Length 29–33″. Average weights: females 9 lbs., males 13⅓ lbs. Plate 48.

3. Falkland Flightless Steamer Duck (*Tachyeres brachypterus*). A Falkland Island species similar to the Flying Steamer Duck but somewhat larger and relatively incapable of flight. Males have a whiter head and females a more reddish head than do the Flying Steamer Ducks. Length 28–32″. Weight 7–9 lbs. Plate 57.

VII. *Tribe Cairinini* (Perching Ducks)

1. Spur-winged Goose (*Plectropterus gambensis*). A large gooselike bird from central and southern Africa, with generally iridescent blackish coloration, bare facial skin in adults, and long bony spurs at the wrists. The sexes are similar, but the female is considerably smaller. The Black Spur-wing is a darker southern

race. Length 30–39″. Average weights: females 7–12 lbs., males 12–15 (but rarely to 22) lbs. Plate 49.

2. Muscovy Duck (*Cairina moschata*). The wild Muscovy is native to tropical Central and South America, usually differing from the domestic varieties by its uniformly dark iridescent coloration except for variably extensive white wing coverts and, in the male, smaller facial caruncles. Length 26–33″. Average weights: females 2¾ lbs., males 6½ lbs. Plate 50.

3. White-winged Wood Duck (*Cairina scutulata*). A southeastern Asian species similar to the preceding one, but with a brown and iridescent blackish body and a black and white speckled head, which is sometimes pure white in males. Length 26–30″. Average weights: females 4¾ to 6¾ lbs., males 7½ to 9½ lbs. Plate 58.

4. Hartlaub's Duck (*Pteronetta hartlaubi*). A central African species with a rich chocolate brown body, blue wing coverts, and a blackish head having a variable amount of white in males. Length 22–23″. Weight 1¾ to 2 lbs. Plate 51.

5. Comb Duck (*Sarkidiornis melanotos*). A South American, African, and south Asian species that is distinguished by the black and white speckled head and white breast of both sexes and, in the much larger males, by a black fatty knob on the bill. Both sexes are dark and iridescent above; the South American race has black flanks also. Length 22–30″. Average weights: females 2⅘ lbs., males 4½ lbs. Plate 52.

6. Green Pygmy Goose (*Nettapus pulchellus*). An East Indian and northern Australian pygmy goose, with finely barred black and white breasts and flanks in both sexes. The male has a green head with white cheeks and throat. Length 13–14″. Average weight (both sexes) 11 ozs. Figure 15.

7. Cotton Pygmy Goose or Cotton Teal (*Nettapus coromandelianus*). A southern Asiatic and northeastern Australian pygmy goose. The male in nuptial plumage is largely white, with a green back, a dark "cap" over the eyes, and a narrow dark "necklace." The female is similar but duller throughout. Both sexes lack the barring of the preceding species. Length 13″. Weight 9–12 ozs. Plate 59.

8. African Pygmy Goose (*Nettapus auritus*). A tiny species of central and southern Africa that is distinguished by the brownish flanks and breast of both sexes and, in males, a beautiful white and green head and an orange-yellow bill. Length 11–12″. Weight (males) 10 ozs. Plate 85.

9. Ringed Teal (*Callonetta leucophrys*). A southeastern South American species (often included in the genus *Anas* with the typical dabbling ducks) that may be distinguished by the large white patch in front of the green speculum and, in males, by the finely speckled pink breast and the buffy head with its black posterior border, which comes forward around the base of the neck to form an incomplete ring. Length 14–15″. Weight 11–12 ozs. Figure 4. Plate 86.

10. North American Wood Duck (*Aix sponsa*). A North American perching duck with marked sexual dimorphism. In nuptial plumage the male, with its long iridescent crest, white throat, and brightly patterned body, is easily identifiable. The female is a mottled gray brown with a broad white eye-ring and throat. Length 17–20″. Average weights: females 1¼ lbs., males 1½ lbs. Plates 61, 87.

11. Mandarin Duck (*Aix galericulata*). An east Asian species even more brightly colored than the preceding species. The male in nuptial plumage has a long crest with broad white central stripe, orange "whiskers," and a pair of very large, orange "sail" feathers that may be erected along the back. The female is similar to the female North American Wood Duck, but has a paler gray head with a narrower white eye-ring. Length 17–20″. Average weights: females 1 lb., males 1⅓ lbs. Figure 7. Plate 88.

12. Australian Wood Duck or Maned Goose (*Chenonetta jubata*). An Australian and Tasmanian perching duck with a diagonal green and white speculum pattern. The male is mostly grayish, with brown head feathers that are lengthened into a short "mane." The female is similar to those of the two preceding species but is larger and has dark stripes through the eye and cheek. Length 19–22″. Average weight (both sexes) 1¾ lbs. Plate 89.

13. Brazilian Teal (*Amazonetta brasiliensis*). A small South American perching duck readily distinguished by red feet and a green and white speculum pattern in both sexes. The male has in addition a bright red bill and an inconspicuous black crest. Length 14–16″. Weight 1¼ to 1⅓ lbs. Plates 60, 90.

VIII. *Tribe Anatini* (Dabbling or Surface-feeding Ducks)

1. Torrent Duck (*Merganetta armata*). A slim-bodied species found only in the Andean streams of South America, probably more closely allied to the perching ducks than to the dabbling ducks, and possibly classifiable as a distinct tribe. Both sexes have red bills and green speculums bordered in front and behind with white. Females are grayish above and a rusty brown below. Males vary greatly in body color in the various races, but in all cases have white heads with a black eye-stripe that divides posteriorly to join a black crown-stripe extending down the back of the head and neck. Length 15–17″. Weight 15 ozs. Figure 15. Plates 62, 91.

2. Blue or Mountain Duck (*Hymenolaimus malacorhynchus*). A New Zealand stream-dwelling species having an overall slate-blue coloration with brown spotting on the breast and flanks. The yellow eyes and bill, the latter with overhanging flaps, are also distinctive. Length 22″. Weight 1¾ lbs. Plate 92.

3. Salvadori's Duck (*Anas waigiuensis*). A secretive species of the New Guinea mountain streams, similar in shape and size to the Torrent Duck. The

speculum pattern is also similar, but both sexes have brown heads and strongly barred black and white body patterns. Length 15–17″. Plate 63.

4. African Black Duck (*Anas sparsa*). A central and southern African forest-dwelling species, almost uniformly black in both sexes except for a Mallard-like speculum and white spots on the back and upper flanks. Length 22–27″. Plate 64.

5. European Wigeon (*Anas penelope*). A Eurasian and rarely North American species of wigeon. Like all wigeon, both sexes have white upper wing coverts and green speculum patterns. The male in nuptial plumage has a bright orange-brown head with a buff-colored forehead and a variable amount of green behind the eyes. Length 17–21″. Average weights: females 1¼ lbs., males 1½ lbs. Plate 93.

6. American Wigeon or Baldpate (*Anas americana*). A North American wigeon in which the male in nuptial plumage is distinguished by a white forehead, green eye-stripe, and lilac breast and flanks. The female also has a more distinctly lilac tone than does the preceding species. Length 18–23″. Average weights: females 1¾ lbs., males 2 lbs. Plate 66.

7. Chiloé Wigeon (*Anas sibilatrix*). A brightly colored wigeon from southern South America, the only species of dabbling duck in which the female exhibits the same iridescent green head coloration as does the male. Both sexes also have orange-brown flanks and a "scaly" black and white breast pattern. Length 21″. Average weights: females 1⅘ lbs., males 2 lbs. Plate 65.

8. Falcated Duck (*Anas falcata*). An east Asian species in which the breeding male has a striking bronze and green crest, a grayish body, and long sickle-shaped inner wing feathers that curve downward. The female generally resembles a female wigeon but lacks the white upper wing coverts. Length 18–21″. Weight 1⅘ lbs. Figure 8. Plate 67.

9. Gadwall (*Anas strepera*). A species widely distributed through the northern hemisphere in the breeding season; the only dabbling duck that has a white speculum pattern. In nuptial plumage the male has a brownish head, a generally gray body, and a black rump, whereas the female is an inconspicuous brown duck with yellow feet and a mottled yellow bill. Length 19–23″. Average weights: females 1¾ lbs., males 2 lbs. Figure 14. Plate 68.

10. Baikal Teal (*Anas formosa*). An east Asian species and one of the most handsome of all ducks. In nuptial plumage the male has a beautiful yellow, green, white, and black head pattern unique among waterfowl, and the female has a concealing brown and buff plumage pattern, with a conspicuous pale buff cheek mark. Length 16″. Weight (males) 18 ozs. Figure 8. Plate 94.

11. Northern Green-winged or European Teal (*Anas crecca*). A northern hemisphere teal of wide temperate zone distribution. Both sexes have a black and green speculum pattern, and males in nuptial plumage have a brown head and

green eye-stripe, which is separated from the brown by a narrow light line. This line and a horizontal white stripe above the wing are absent in the American race. Instead, such males have a vertical white line between the flank and breast. Length 13–16″. Average weights: females 11 ozs., males 13 ozs. Plate 69.

12. South American Green-winged Teal or Speckled Teal (*Anas flavirostris*). A brownish teal of various parts of western and southern South America. It is about the size of the preceding species and has the same green and black speculum pattern. Both sexes are generally pale brownish, with darker brown heads and sometimes with yellow bills ("Yellow-billed Teal"), but gray in the north Andean races. Length 15–17″. Weight 14–15 ozs. Figure 8. Plate 70.

13. Cape Teal (*Anas capensis*). A central and south African teal with a green and black speculum that is bordered broadly with white in front and behind. Both sexes are a pale, mottled gray throughout, with pink bills and reddish eyes. Length 15″. Plate 95.

14. Gray Teal (*Anas gibberifrons*). An East Indian, Australian, and New Zealand teal, both sexes of which are almost uniformly grayish brown except for their green and black speculum patterns bordered with white. Like the preceding species, both sexes have reddish eyes. Length 16″. Average weights: females 1 lb., males $1\frac{1}{8}$ lbs. Plate 71.

15. Madagascan Teal (*Anas bernieri*). A reddish "variant" of the Gray Teal that is limited to western Madagascar. The blackish speculum lacks iridescence and the bill and legs are reddish. Length 16″. Figure 3.

16. Chestnut Teal (*Anas castanea*). An Australian and Tasmanian teal similar in size and speculum pattern to the Gray Teal, but the male has an iridescent green head and a chestnut-colored breast and flanks. Both sexes have red eyes, but females can be distinguished from Gray Teal by their generally darker brown coloration. Length 16″. Average weights: females $1\frac{1}{10}$ lbs., males $1\frac{1}{8}$ lbs. Plate 72.

17. Brown Teal (*Anas aucklandica*). A rare teal of New Zealand and adjacent islands that is similar in most respects to the preceding species, but that has brown eyes, pale eye-rings, and a longer tail. Males vary greatly in their relative brightness, with some approaching the Chestnut Teal pattern and others similar in appearance to the female. The two island races are practically flightless. Length 17–19″. Plate 73.

18. Mallard (*Anas platyrhynchos*). The most familiar and possibly most abundant duck throughout most of the northern hemisphere. The male Common Mallard (*A. p. platyrhynchos*) in nuptial plumage is widely familiar, and the brown female with its purple and white-bordered speculum is also well known. Males of the smaller (16–20″) Hawaiian and Laysan Island races (Figure 3) generally resemble females, and older males often are albinistic on the head. In Mexico and the southern United States, various sedentary races of Mallards occur (Mexican

Duck, Florida Duck, Mottled Duck), in which the males closely resemble the brown females. Length 21–26". Average weights: (Florida Duck) females 1¾ lbs., males 2½ lbs.; (Common Mallard) females 2½ lbs., males 2¾ lbs. Plate 74.

19. American Black Duck (*Anas rubripes*). A Mallardlike duck of eastern North America. Because the male closely resembles the female, and both sexes are much darker than female Mallards, this species is readily distinguishable from the preceding one. Hybrid combinations with Mallards are frequent in the eastern states. Length 21–26". Average weights: females 2½ lbs., males 2¾ lbs. Plate 76.

20. Meller's Duck (*Anas melleri*). A large Madagascan species in which both sexes resemble the female Mallard except for their black bills and green speculums. Length 25–27". Figure 3.

21. Yellow-billed Duck (*Anas undulata*). A central and south African Mallardlike species in which the sexes are nearly identical, with dark blackish plumage and yellow bills that are slightly brighter in males. Length 21–22". Weight 1⅘ to 2⅙ lbs. Plate 77.

22. Spot-billed Duck (*Anas poecilorhyncha*). An Australasian species varying in appearance from the light grayish Indian race with its yellow-tipped bill, through the darker Chinese race with its slightly streaked cheeks, to the darkest New Zealand "Gray Duck" and Australian "Black Duck" with their distinctive cheek-stripes. These last two forms are sometimes considered a separate species (*A. superciliosa*). In all these, the males and females are similar in appearance. Length 24". Average weights: females 2¼ lbs., males 2½ lbs. Plates 78, 79.

23. Philippine Duck (*Anas luzonica*). A Mallardlike species found only in the Philippine Islands; both sexes are uniformly gray except for brown heads and darker eye-stripes. Length 19–23". Plate 80.

24. Bronze-winged Duck (*Anas specularis*). A species of southern South America, in which both sexes are alike and exhibit, in addition to the brilliant bronze speculum, a white facial crescent and a white throat. The dark brown crescent-shaped spots on the flanks are also distinctive. Length 21". Plate 81.

25. Crested Duck (*Anas specularioides*). A slim-bodied species occurring mainly on the high Andean lakes of southern South America, similar in general appearance and speculum color to the preceding species, but with a dark brown crest and an elongated tail in both sexes. Sometimes the species is considered an aberrant shelduck (*Lophonetta*). Length 20–24". Average weights: females 2 lbs., males 2½ lbs. Plate 97.

26. Pintail (*Anas acuta*). An abundant species found throughout much of the northern hemisphere and occurring also on the subantarctic Kerguelen and Crozet Islands (Figure 3). In nuptial plumage the male Northern Pintail's (*A. a. acuta*) elongated tail, brown head, and white breast and underparts are distinctive.

Females and males of the two smaller (17–25″) island races are brownish, with slate-blue bills and feet, and less iridescent bronze speculum patterns. Length 20–29″. Average weights: (Northern race) females 1¾ lbs., males 2¼ lbs. Figure 8. Plate 82.

27. Yellow-billed or Brown Pintail (*Anas georgica*). A brownish pintail of South America and adjacent islands (Figure 3), in which the sexes are alike, with uniformly brown bodies and yellow bills. Length 20–21″. Average weights: females 1½ lbs., males 1⁷⁄₁₀ lbs. Plate 83.

28. Bahama Pintail (*Anas bahamensis*). A West Indian and South American pintail differing from the preceding species by its white cheeks and the brightly colored red and blue bill, which is duller in females. The buffy tips of the second-aries, typical of all pintails, form a broad posterior border to the green speculum. Length 18–20″. Weight 1½ lbs. Figure 8. Plate 84.

29. Red-billed Pintail (*Anas erythrorhyncha*). A grayish African pintail similar to the preceding species except for the entirely red bill of both sexes. The buffy secondary tips are so broad that they essentially replace the metallic speculum. In addition, the body feathers have a paler, less brownish color than in the preceding species. Length 17″. Plate 117.

30. Silver Teal (*Anas versicolor*). A South American teal of both the Andes ("Puna Teal") and the southern lowlands ("Versicolor Teal"). The sexes are alike, with dark "caps" extending over their eyes, variably bluish bills, and vertical gray barring on the flanks. The intensity of the barring and bill coloration varies in the different races. Length 16–19″. Average weights: (Versicolor race) females 13 ozs., males 1 lb. Plate 118.

31. Hottentot Teal (*Anas punctata*). A tiny African and Madagascan teal, similar to the preceding species in that both sexes have blue bills and "capped" heads; in addition, a dark brown "thumbprint" is present in the ear region. Length 12–13″. Weight 8–9 ozs. Plate 119.

32. Garganey (*Anas querquedula*). A Eurasian teal with gray forewing coverts and a green speculum. The male in nuptial plumage has a reddish brown head with broad white "eyebrows" extending back to the nape. The female is an inconspicuous brown bird not easily separated from other female "blue-winged ducks," but it has grayish rather than bluish wing coverts. The wooden, rattling voice of the male is distinctive. Length 15″. Average weights: females 12 ozs., males 1 lb. Plate 120.

33. Blue-winged Teal (*Anas discors*). A North American teal with light blue wing coverts and a green speculum in both sexes. The male in nuptial plumage has a bluish gray head and white facial crescent extending back over the eyes, while the rest of the body is a spotted brown. The species winters as far

south as central South America. Length 14–16″. Average weights: females 13 ozs., males 1 lb. Plate 121.

34. Cinnamon Teal (*Anas cyanoptera*). A teal that extends through much of western North America and much of South America. Although similar to the preceding species in its light blue wing coverts and green speculum, the male in nuptial plumage is a rich reddish-brown throughout, except for a black rump. The female is similar to the female Blue-winged Teal but is slightly more rust-colored, having a longer, more shovelerlike bill. Length 15–19″. Average weights: (N. American race) females 13 ozs., males 1 lb. Plate 122.

35. Red Shoveler (*Anas platalea*). A southern South American blue-winged duck with a shovelerlike bill. The male is a reddish-brown, spotted bird with a lighter, grayish head and pale eyes. The female is brown and, like the male, has a long pointed tail. Length 21″. Average weights: females 1⅐ lbs., males 1⅓ lbs. Plate 123.

36. Cape Shoveler (*Anas smithi*). A shoveler limited to southern Africa. The male is of a mottled brown color over most of the body, with a lighter head and a pale yellow iris. The female is similar, but has a browner body and a dark brown iris. Length 20″. Plates 124, 127.

37. Australasian Shoveler (*Anas rhynchotis*). A species limited to southern Australia, Tasmania, and New Zealand. Like all shovelers it has blue upper wing coverts and a green speculum pattern in both sexes, but the male is unique in its slate-blue bill and white facial crescent (sometimes seen in molting Northern Shovelers). Males of the New Zealand race are generally more brightly colored than those of the Australian form, and females of both closely resemble female Northern Shovelers. Length 18–22″. Average weight (both sexes) 1½ lbs. Figure 8. Plate 125.

38. Northern or Common Shoveler (*Anas clypeata*). The most widely distributed species of shoveler, found over much of the northern hemisphere. In nuptial plumage the male is the most colorful of all shovelers, with an iridescent green head, a white breast, and reddish-brown flanks. The female is an inconspicuous brown. Length 17–22″. Average weights: females 1¼ lbs., males 1½ lbs. Plate 126.

39. Pink-eared Duck (*Malacorhynchus membranaceus*). A shovelerlike Australian and Tasmanian species with an unusual soft flap hanging from the end of the elongated bill. Both sexes have identical vertically barred gray plumage, and conspicuous dark eye-stripes. The pink ear-marks are usually not visible. Length 15–16″. Average weights: females 12 ozs., males 14 ozs. Plate 98.

40. Marbled Teal (*Marmaronetta angustirostris*). A teal-like duck (usually included in the genus *Anas*), ranging from the Mediterranean area to south-western Asia. Both sexes have a pale mottled grayish-brown plumage throughout.

A dark eye-stripe and small crest similar to those of the larger Crested Duck occurs in both sexes, while the male has a narrow light stripe near the tip of its bill. Length 15″. Weight 17 ozs. Plate 99.

IX. *Tribe Aythyini* (Pochards)

1. Pink-headed Duck (*Rhodonessa caryophyllacea*). A species that is probably extinct, once found in northeastern and eastern India and Nepal. Both sexes had a dark brownish black body and lighter wings. The head and neck plumage of the male was an extraordinary bright pink; that of the female, somewhat paler. Length 22″. Weight 2–2¼ lbs. Figure 14.

2. Red-crested Pochard (*Netta rufina*). A pochard of southern and eastern Europe, ranging east to central Asia. The male is unique in having a bright orange "shaving brush" crest and red bill. The female's plumage is a rather uniform brown, but the upper half of the head is distinctly darker than the lower portion. In both sexes a pale wing-stripe extends to the outer primaries. Length 22″. Average weights: females 2⅛ lbs., males 2½ lbs. Plate 100.

3. Southern Pochard (*Netta erythropthalma*). A pochard of northern South America and eastern and southern Africa. The male is a generally dark bird, with brownish flanks, a black breast, and a dark purplish head. The female is also generally dark brown except for a white wing-stripe and pale marks on the cheeks and behind the eyes. Length 20″. Weight 1¾–2¼ lbs. Plate 128.

4. Rosy-billed Pochard (*Netta peposaca*). A pochard restricted to southern South America, except the extreme southern portions. The male has a unique bright red bill with a bulbous basal enlargement; otherwise, the head is iridescent purple and the body is generally gray and black. The female is a relatively uniform brown, with lighter undertail coverts and a white wing-stripe. Length 22″. Average weights: females 2⅕ lbs., males 2¾ lbs. Plate 129.

5. Canvasback (*Aythya valisineria*). A large North American pochard noted for its long bill and sloping forehead profile. The male in nuptial plumage has a dark reddish-brown head, a black breast, and grayish-white flanks and back. The female is pale grayish-brown. Length 19–24″. Average weights: females 2¾ lbs., males 3 lbs. Plate 130.

6. European Pochard (*Aythya ferina*). A European and Asian pochard remarkably similar to the preceding species, except for a shorter bill and higher head profile and a light terminal band across the bill of the male. In both sexes the color and body form is generally intermediate between those of the Canvasback and Redhead. Length 18–23″. Average weights: females 2¼ lbs., males 2½ lbs. Plate 131.

7. Redhead (*Aythya americana*). A North American pochard similar to, but smaller than, the Canvasback. Males have a brighter reddish head, a darker gray body with a more extensive black breast, and a more rounded head profile. The female is a generally nondescript brown and has an indistinct eye-ring. Length 18–22″. Average weights: females $2\frac{1}{4}$ lbs., males $2\frac{1}{2}$ lbs. Plate 101.

8. Ring-necked Duck (*Aythya collaris*). A North American pochard especially fond of forested ponds. In nuptial plumage the male's combination of a blackish breast and back, with white stripes at both the base and near the tip of the bill, is distinctive. The female is brownish, with a light stripe near the tip of her bill. She also has a distinct pale eye-ring and posterior eye-stripe. Length 15–18″. Average weights: females $1\frac{1}{2}$ lbs., males $1\frac{3}{4}$ lbs. Plate 132.

9. Australasian White-eye (*Aythya australis*). A pochard of Australia, New Zealand, and adjacent islands. It is generally brownish, except for the white abdomen, wing-stripes, and undertail coverts typical of this group. Both sexes can be distinguished from related species by the broad light tip of the bill. As in other species of this group, females can be recognized by their brown eyes. Length 18″. Average weights: females $1\frac{3}{5}$ lbs., males $1\frac{3}{4}$ lbs. Plate 133.

10. Baer's Pochard (*Aythya baeri*). An east Siberian pochard of the old world white-eye group, collectively noted for the white iris color in the males. The sexes are quite similar and, like all species of white-eyes, have brown breasts and flanks, white abdomens, white undertail coverts, and white wing-stripes. This species differs from other pochards in having iridescent green on the head, though it is of limited extent in females, which also have brown eyes. Length 18″. Plate 134.

11. Ferruginous or Common White-eye (*Aythya nyroca*). A southern Eurasian pochard that is generally chestnut-colored over most of its body. Unlike the preceding species it has a uniformly dark bill and is more ruddy in general tone. Length 16″. Average weights: females $1\frac{1}{4}$ lbs., males $1\frac{1}{3}$ lbs. Plate 135.

12. Madagascan White-eye (*Aythya innotata*). An eastern Madagascan pochard that is clearly a close relative of the last species, differing from it in its somewhat larger size and darker body coloration. Length 18″. Figure 3.

13. New Zealand Scaup (*Aythya novae-seelandiae*). A pochard limited to New Zealand and adjacent islands. Like all scaup, the female is generally dark brown. The male is the darkest of the pochards, being iridescent green or black throughout, except for the white wing markings. Length 18″. Plate 136.

14. Tufted Duck (*Aythya fuligula*). A Eurasian pochard, the male of which is similar to the Ring-necked Duck, undoubtedly a member of the scaup group. Females have a small white mark behind the bill and the white wing-stripe typical of this group, but are otherwise dark brown. The male is the only pochard that

has a distinctly lengthened crest; otherwise, it is scauplike. Length 17–18″. Average weights: females 1½ lbs., males 1¾ lbs. Plate 102.

15. Greater Scaup (*Aythya marila*). The only pochard occurring both in North America and Eurasia, perhaps because of its maritime wintering habitat. The female is a uniform brown except for a whitish patch behind the bill (and in the ear region during summer) and the usual white wing-stripe. The male in nuptial plumage has an iridescent green head, a black breast, a pale gray back, and immaculate white flanks. Length 16–20″. Average weights: females 2 lbs., males 2⅕ lbs. Figure 7. Plate 103.

16. Lesser Scaup (*Aythya affinis*). A near relative of the last species, but restricted to North America. Females of the two scaups are almost identical, but the white wing-stripes are not quite so extensive in both sexes of this species. The male in nuptial plumage can be distinguished by its iridescent purple head and its generally higher head profile, as well as its more grayish back and flanks. Length 15–19″. Average weights: females 1⅘ lbs., males 2 lbs. Plate 137.

X. *Tribe Mergini* (Sea Ducks)

1. Common Eider (*Somateria mollissima*). The most abundant and widely distributed eider, breeding along most of the arctic coasts of the northern hemisphere. Like the other large eiders, Common Eiders are bulky birds with strong bills. In nuptial plumage the males may be easily recognized by the broad black stripe extending across the eyes from the bill to the nape. Much of the area below and behind the eyes is an unusual, pigmented green color. Females are generally brown and somewhat Mallardlike, but lack an iridescent speculum and have dark brown vertical barring on the flanks. Length 22–28″. Average weights: females 3⅔ lbs., males 4½ lbs. (Pacific race averages 5⅓ and 5¾ lbs.) Plate 104.

2. King Eider (*Somateria spectabilis*). This eider breeds on the arctic coasts of North America, Europe, and Asia. The male in nuptial plumage has a fatty, orange frontal enlargement at the base of the red bill; the rest of the head is mostly pale blue and green. In much the same manner as the two preceding species, the body color consists mostly of contrasting areas of black and white. The female is similar to those of the other large eiders, except that it lacks vertical flank barring and has instead Mallardlike crescent-shaped markings. Length 19–25″. Average weights: females 3¾ lbs., males 4 lbs. Figure 9. Plate 105.

3. Spectacled Eider (*Somateria fischeri*). The rarest eider and the one that is the most limited in distribution, breeding only in northwestern Alaska and adjacent Siberia. The male in nuptial plumage is unique in possessing white "spectacles" surrounded by green feathers. The female is much like the female Common Eider but has a pair of "spectacles" faintly outlined around the eyes. Length 20–23″. Average weights: females 3½ lbs., males 3¾ lbs. Figure 9. Plate 106.

4. Steller's Eider (*Polysticta stelleri*). This species, the smallest of the eiders, breeds in coastal Alaska and extreme northern Asia. The male in nuptial plumage is a strikingly handsome bird, with a predominantly white head, a black throat, neck, and back, and a rich chestnut breast, abdomen, and flanks. Unlike the other eiders, both sexes have an iridescent purple speculum bordered with white; otherwise, the female is uniformly dark brown. Length 17–19". Weight (both sexes) $1\frac{9}{10}$–$2\frac{1}{10}$ lbs. Figure 4. Plate 107.

5. Labrador Duck (*Camptorhynchus labradorius*). An extinct sea duck that occurred along the northeast coast of North America. The male had black and white plumage, with a distinctive flap-edged bill that was black except for a yellow stripe. The female was generally grayish brown, with white wing markings. Length 20". Figure 14.

6. Harlequin Duck (*Histrionicus histrionicus*). A coastal and stream-dwelling bird extensively distributed through the northern parts of the northern hemisphere, though rarely abundant anywhere except along coastal Alaska and Iceland. The name Harlequin well describes the male in nuptial plumage; it is mostly slate blue with bizarre stripes and spots of white, with chestnut flanks. The female is dark brown except for pale spots above and below the eyes and in the ear region. Length 15–21". Average weights: females $1\frac{1}{4}$ lbs., males $1\frac{1}{2}$ lbs. Figure 4. Plate 138.

7. Long-tailed Duck or Oldsquaw (*Clangula hyemalis*). A high-arctic sea duck breeding through most of the northern tundra regions, wintering along temperate zone coastlines and on large, deep lakes. In any plumage the adult male has a black breast and an elongated tail; seasonally it has variable amounts of white and black in its plumage. The female lacks the long tail and has a somewhat piebald appearance, with a mixture of white, brown, and blackish feathers. Length 15–23". Average weights: females $1\frac{1}{2}$ lbs., males $1\frac{3}{4}$ lbs. Plate 108.

8. Black Scoter (*Melanitta nigra*). A sea duck that is found over the coasts of much of the northern hemisphere, but that has a limited breeding range in arctic North America. The adult male is uniformly glossy black, with a bill that is variably enlarged basally and decorated with yellow, which is most extensive in the American race that breeds in western Alaska. The female is a uniformly dark brown except for paler cheeks, neck, and throat. Length 17–21". Average weights: females $2\frac{1}{4}$ lbs., males $2\frac{1}{2}$ lbs. Plate 109.

9. Surf Scoter (*Melanitta perspicillata*). A sea duck of limited breeding distribution in arctic America, that winters along both North American coastlines. The male's plumage is black, except for white forehead and nape patches, and a bill that is a bright combination of white, yellow, red, and black. The female is uniformly brown except for lighter markings in the cheek, ear, and nape

regions. Length 17–21″. Average weights: females 2 lbs., males $2\frac{1}{4}$ lbs. Figure 4. Plate 139.

10. White-winged Scoter (*Melanitta fusca*). A sea duck breeding widely over the temperate and arctic parts of the northern hemisphere, wintering on the coasts. It breeds on inland marshes often surprisingly far from salt water. The male is black except for white wing patches and a white stripe behind the white eyes. The female closely resembles the female Surf Scoter, but has white wing patches. Length 19–24″. Average weights: females $2\frac{3}{4}$ lbs., males $3\frac{1}{2}$ lbs. Figure 4. Plate 140.

11. Bufflehead (*Bucephala albeola*). A fresh-water diving duck that is small enough to occupy abandoned woodpecker cavities in Canada and the northern states. The male in nuptial plumage is mostly white, with a dark back and a large head that is dark and iridescent except for a triangular white crest. The grayish female has a brown head with a white patch extending from the eye to the ear region. Length 13–16″. Average weights: females 12 ozs., males 1 lb. Figure 9. Plates 110, 141.

12. Barrow's Goldeneye (*Bucephala islandica*). A western North American hole-nesting duck that also occurs in Labrador, Iceland, and Greenland. The male in nuptial plumage is mainly black and white, with an iridescent purple head except for a white facial crescent. The female has an entirely brown head and a gray to white body, often exhibiting a completely yellow bill. Length 16–20″. Average weights: females $1\frac{3}{5}$ lbs., males $2\frac{2}{5}$ lbs. Figure 4. Plate 142.

13. Common Goldeneye (*Bucephala ciangula*). The most widely distributed species of goldeneye, nesting in hollow trees and cavities among the coniferous woodlands of the northern hemisphere. The male in nuptial plumage differs from the Barrow's Goldeneye in having a green-glossed head with a circular white patch and a more extensive white wing patch. The female is not always certainly distinguished from the female Barrow's, having a head profile that is higher and more pointed than that of the "flat-topped" Barrow's and having little or no yellow on its bill. Length 16–20″. Average weights: females $1\frac{3}{4}$ lbs., males $2\frac{1}{5}$ lbs. Figures 9, 12. Plates 111, 142.

14. Hooded Merganser (*Mergus cucullatus*). A North American hole-nesting merganser that is especially fond of woodland ponds and streams. The male in nuptial plumage has a long, rounded white crest trimmed at the tip with black. The female, also crested, is generally grayish to brownish, with small white wing markings. Length 16–19″. Average weights: females $1\frac{1}{4}$ lbs., males $1\frac{1}{2}$ lbs. Figure 9. Plate 112.

15. Smew (*Mergus albellus*). A small merganser of Europe and Asia, with a shorter bill than that of the preceding species. The male in nuptial plumage is mostly white, with a black nape "V" and a small black "mask." The female's

body is gray, and her head is brown above, sharply contrasting with the white below. Length 14–16″. Weight $1\frac{1}{8}$–$1\frac{5}{8}$ lbs. Plate 143.

16. Brazilian Merganser (*Mergus octosetaceus*). A rare merganser restricted to southern Brazil and adjacent Paraguay and northeastern Argentina. Both sexes have iridescent green heads with long, narrow crests; and both are generally dark-colored except for white wing markings. Length 20″ (estimated). Figure 15.

17. Red-breasted Merganser (*Mergus serrator*). A merganser that is widely distributed throughout North America, Europe, and Asia. In nuptial plumage the male is easily distinguished by its reddish-brown breast that is separated from the narrowly crested green head by a white neck-ring. The female has a similarly crested brown head, which shades gradually into a paler throat. Length 19–26″. Average weights: females 2 lbs., males $2\frac{1}{2}$ lbs. Figure 9. Plate 144.

18. Chinese Merganser (*Mergus squamatus*). An east Asian merganser about which very little is known. The male generally resembles that of the preceding species, but has a white breast and a "scaly" flank pattern. The female closely resembles the female Red-breasted Merganser. Length 22″ (estimated). Figure 15.

19. Goosander or Common Merganser (*Mergus merganser*). The largest merganser, and one that is widely distributed in Eurasia and North America ("American Merganser"). In nuptial plumage the male has a salmon-tinted white body and a slightly crested green head. The female has a shaggy crest like that of the Red-breasted Merganser, but the white throat pattern is more sharply defined. Length 21–27″. Average weights: females $2\frac{1}{2}$ lbs., males $3\frac{1}{2}$ lbs. Plate 113.

20. Auckland Island Merganser (*Mergus australis*). An extinct merganser that occurred on the Auckland Islands. Both sexes were dull-colored with crested brown heads and gray bodies. Length 23″. Figure 14.

XI. *Tribe Oxyurini* (Stiff-tailed Ducks)

1. Black-headed Duck (*Heteronetta atricapilla*). A teal-sized duck of southern South America, though not the extreme south, with characteristics of both dabbling ducks and stiff-tails. The male is uniformly brown, except for a black head and a seasonally blue bill that is reddish at the base. The female somewhat resembles a female Cinnamon Teal, but lacks an iridescent speculum. The tail is not stiffened or elongated, and diving is infrequent. Length 14–15″. Average weights: females $1\frac{1}{4}$ lbs., males $1\frac{1}{6}$ lbs. Plate 114.

2. Masked Duck (*Oxyura dominica*). The only stiff-tail with white wing-patches; limited in range to the West Indies and tropical parts of Central and South America. The breeding male has a blue bill and a black facial mask but is otherwise mostly a ruddy brown; the brownish female is distinguished by pale

lines above and below the dark eye-stripe. Length 12–14″. Average weights: females 13 ozs., males 14–15 oz. Figure 15. Plate 145.

3. Ruddy Duck (*Oxyura jamaicensis*). A species of stiff-tail extending from North America through Central and South America along the Andes and also to the West Indies. In all races the breeding male has a bright blue bill and a ruddy body; the female is a dingy brown with streaked cheeks. In the North American Ruddy Duck (*O. j. rubida*) the cheeks of the male are white, but in the larger South American races they are mottled or entirely black. Length 14–19″. Average weights: (North American race) females 1 lb., males 1⅖ lbs. Plate 115.

4. White-headed Duck (*Oxyura leucocephala*). A stiff-tail found locally in various parts of the Mediterranean region, the Middle East, and in central Asia. It is somewhat similar to the above species, but larger. The male White-headed Duck has a more bulbous blue bill, with the white cheeks extending up over the eyes and bill. Length 18″. Average weights: females 1⅗lbs., males 1⅘ lbs. Figure 15.

5. Argentine Ruddy Duck (*Oxyura vittata*). A stiff-tail found in the lowland marshes of southern South America. Although similar to the other South American Ruddy Ducks, the Argentine species is smaller, the bill is narrower, and the female has a distinctly streaked cheek pattern. Length 16″. Weight 1¼ to 1⅓ lbs. Plate 146.

6. Maccoa Duck (*Oxyura maccoa*). A stiff-tail limited to eastern and southern Africa. The male in breeding plumage is of a uniform ruddy color throughout, except for its white undertail coverts and an entirely black head. Males are not easily distinguished from the Australian and South American stiff-tails, although they are a rustier brown and both sexes have basally enlarged bills. Length 16–18″. Plate 147.

7. Australian Blue-billed Duck (*Oxyura australis*). A stiff-tail found in southern Australia and Tasmania. Males in breeding plumage have entirely black heads and rusty-brown bodies; the brownish female's cheeks are indistinctly freckled and mottled. Length 14–16″. Average weights: females 1⅘ lbs., males 1¾ lbs. Plate 148.

8. Musk Duck (*Biziura lobata*). A very large stiff-tail from southern Australia and Tasmania, exhibiting marked sexual differences in body size. The adult male is unique among waterfowl in possessing a pendant skin-fold that hangs down below the bill like a wattle. This appendage is rudimentary in females, but both sexes are identically barred dark gray and black, totally lacking the ruddy color of the other true stiff-tails. In common with the more typical species, however, the male frequently cocks his tail, especially during display. Length 24–29″. Average weights: females 3⅖ lbs., males 5¼ lbs. Plate 116.

Selected Bibliography

ALTHOUGH the following references are regarded as especially pertinent for supplementary reading, numerous additional references can be found in the fourth volume of Delacour's *Waterfowl of the World* (over 900 references up to about 1962), in Phillips' *Natural History of the Ducks* (over 2,700 references through 1924), and in N. Kuroda's *Bibliography of the Duck Tribe* (over 6,500 references through 1940). The U. S. Fish and Wildlife Service's *Wildlife Review* has abstracted over 1,900 references on waterfowl from 1935 through 1966. The *Aves* section of *Zoological Record* (Zoological Society of London) annually indexes most English-language publications that concern the Anatidae, and the most recently published volume (covering 1964 literature) has more than 200 references dealing wholly or in part with species of this family.

CHAPTER 1

GENERAL REFERENCES ON THE ANATIDAE

Boyd, Hugh, and Scott, Peter (eds.). *Annual Reports of the Wildfowl Trust.* 18 vols. Slimbridge, England: The Wildfowl Trust, 1950–67.

Delacour, Jean. *The Waterfowl of the World.* 4 vols. London: Country Life, 1954–64.

Johnsgard, P. A. *Handbook of Waterfowl Behavior*. Ithaca, N.Y.: Cornell University Press, 1965.

Kortright, F. H. *The Ducks, Geese, and Swans of North America*. Washington, D.C.: American Wildlife Institute, 1943.

Millais, J. G. *The Natural History of the British Surface-feeding Ducks*. London: Longmans Green, 1902.

————. *British Diving Ducks*. 2 vols. London: Longmans Green, 1913.

Phillips, J. C. *The Natural History of the Ducks*. 4 vols. Boston: Houghton Mifflin, 1922–1926.

Wetmore, Alexander (ed.). *Water, Prey, and Game Birds of North America*. Washington, D.C.: National Geographic Society, 1965.

CHAPTER 2

Distribution and Migrations

Aldrich, J. W., *et al.*, "Migration of Some North American Waterfowl: A Progress Report on an Analysis of Banding Records," *Special Scientific Report: Wildlife*, U. S. Department of the Interior, Fish and Wildlife Service, No. 1. Washington, D.C.: Government Printing Office, 1949.

Atkinson-Willes, G. L. (ed.). *Wildfowl in Great Britain*. No. 3. London: Monographs of the Nature Conservancy, 1963.

Bellrose, F. (1958). "Celestial Orientation by Wild Mallards," *Bird Banding*, 29: 75–90.

Hamilton, W. J., III. (1962). "Celestial Orientation in Juvenal Waterfowl," *Condor*, 64: 19–33.

Hochbaum, H. A. *Travels and Traditions of Waterfowl*. Minneapolis: University of Minnesota Press, 1955.

Matthews, G. V. T. (1961). "'Nonsense' Orientation in Mallard (*Anas platyrhynchos*) and Its Relation to Experiments on Bird Navigation," *Ibis*, 103a: 211–220.

Weller, M. W. (1964). "Distribution and Migration of the Redhead," *Journal of Wildlife Management*, 28: 64–103.

CHAPTER 3

Ecology, Food, and General Behavior

Cottam, C. *Food Habits of North American Diving Ducks*. (Technical Bulletin, U. S. Department of Agriculture, No. 643.) Washington, D.C.: Government Printing Office, 1939.

Keith, L. B. "A Study of Waterfowl Ecology on Small Impoundments in Southeastern Alberta," *Wildlife Monographs*, No. 6, 1961.

McKinney, F. (1965). "The Comfort Movements of Anatidae," *Behaviour*, 25: 120–220.

Martin, A. C., *et al. American Wildlife and Plants*. New York: McGraw-Hill, 1951.

Oring, L. W. (1964). "Behavior and Ecology of Certain Ducks During the Postbreeding Season," *Journal of Wildlife Management*, 28: 223–233.

Yocom, C. F. *Waterfowl and Their Food Plants in Washington*. Seattle: University of Washington Press, 1951.

CHAPTER 4

Sound Production

Humphrey, P. S., and Clark, G. A., Jr. "The Anatomy of Waterfowl," in *The Waterfowl of the World*, Vol. 4. London: Country Life, 1964.

Johnsgard, P. A. "Tracheal Anatomy of the Anatidae and Its Taxonomic Significance," *Twelfth Annual Report of the Wildfowl Trust*. Slimbridge, England: The Wildfowl Trust, 1961.

Sutherland, S. A., and McChesney, D. S. "Sound Production in Two Species of Geese," *The Living Bird, Fourth Annual Report of the Cornell Laboratory of Ornithology*, 1965.

CHAPTER 5

Social Behavior

Dane, B., Walcott, C., and Drury, W. H. (1959). "The Form and Duration of the Display Actions of the Goldeneye (*Bucephala clangula*)," *Behaviour*, 14: 265–281.

Dane, B., and van der Kloot, W. G. (1964). "An Analysis of the Displays of the Goldeneye Duck (*Bucephala clangula* L.)," *Behaviour*, 22: 282–328.

Johnsgard, P. A. (1960). "A Quantitative Study of Sexual Behavior of Mallards and Black Ducks," *Wilson Bulletin*, 72: 133–145.

———. "Comparative Behaviour of the Anatidae and Its Evolutionary Implications," *Eleventh Annual Report of the Wildfowl Trust*. Slimbridge, England: The Wildfowl Trust, 1960.

———. (1960). "Pair-Formation Mechanisms in *Anas* (Anatidae) and Related Genera," *Ibis*, 102: 616–618.

————. "Evolutionary Trends in the Behaviour and Morphology of the Anatidae," *Thirteenth Annual Report of the Wildfowl Trust*. Slimbridge, England:
The Wildfowl Trust, 1962.

————. (1964). "The Sexual Behavior and Systematic Position of the Hooded
Merganser," *Wilson Bulletin*, 73: 226–236.

————. (1964). "Comparative Behavior and Relationships of the Eiders,"
Condor, 66: 113–129.

————. (1966). "Displays of the Australian Musk Duck and Blue-billed Duck,"
Auk, 87: 98–110.

Lorenz, K. Z. (1951–1953). "Comparative Studies on the Behaviour of the
Anatinae," *Avicultural Magazine*, 57: 157–182; 58: 8–17, 61–72, 86–94,
172–184; 59: 24–34, 80–91.

McKinney, F. (1961). "An Analysis of the Displays of the European Eider
Somateria mollissima mollissima (Linneaus) and the Pacific Eider *Somateria
mollissima v. nigra* Bonaparte," *Behaviour*, Suppl. VII.

————. (1965). "The Spring Behavior of Wild Steller's Eiders," *Condor*,
64: 273–290.

Myres, M. T. (1959). "Display Behavior of Bufflehead, Scoters, and Goldeneyes
at Copulation," *Wilson Bulletin*, 71: 159–168.

Raitasuo, K. (1964). "Social Behaviour of the Mallard, *Anas platyrhynchos*, in the
Course of the Annual Cycle," *Papers on Game Research* (Helsinki), 24: 1–72.

Smith, R. I. "The Social Aspects of Reproductive Behavior in the Pintail (*Anas
acuta acuta* L.)." Unpublished Ph.D. dissertation, Utah State University,
1963.

Wood, J. S. (1965). "Some Associations of Behavior to Reproductive Develop-
Development in Canada Geese," *Journal of Wildlife Management*, 29: 237–244.

CHAPTER 6

BREEDING BIOLOGY

Bellrose, F. C., *et al.*, (1961). "Sex Ratios and Age Ratios in North American
Ducks," *Bulletin Illinois Natural History Survey*, 27: 385–474.

Brakhage, G. K. (1965). "Biology and Behavior of Tub-nesting Canada Geese,"
Journal of Wildlife Management, 29: 751–771.

Collias, N. E., and Jahn, L. R. (1959). "Social Behavior and Breeding Success
in Canada Geese (*Branta canadensis*) under Semi-natural Conditions," *Auk*,
76: 478–509.

Cooch, Graham (1961). "Ecological Aspects of the Blue-Snow Goose Complex,"
Auk, 78: 72–89.

Craighead, J. J., and Stockstag, D. S. (1964). "Breeding Age of Canada Geese," *Journal of Wildlife Management*, 28: 57–64.

Duebbert, H. F. (1966). "Island Nesting of the Gadwall in North Dakota," *Wilson Bulletin*, 78: 12–25.

Dzubin, Alex. "Some Evidences of Home Range in Waterfowl," *Transactions of the Twentieth North American Wildlife Conference*, 1955.

Frith, H. J. "Ecology of Wild Ducks in Inland Australia," in *Biogeography and Ecology in Australia*. Den Haag: W. Junk, 1959.

Lebret, T. (1961). "The Pair-Formation in the Annual Cycle of the Mallard, *Anas platyrhynchos* L.," *Ardea*, 49: 97–158.

McKinney, F. "Spacing and Chasing in Breeding Ducks," *Sixteenth Annual Report of the Wildfowl Trust*. Slimbridge, England: The Wildfowl Trust, 1965.

Weller, M. W. (1965). "Chronology of Pair Formation in Some Nearctic *Aythya* (Anatidae)," *Auk*, 82: 227–235.

———. (1959). "Parasitic Egg Laying in the Redhead (*Aythya americana*) and Other North American Anatidae," *Ecological Monographs*, 29: 333–365.

———. "The Reproductive Cycle," in *The Waterfowl of the World*, Vol. 4. London: Country Life, 1964.

CHAPTER 7

Molts and Plumages

Carney, S. M. "Preliminary Keys of Waterfowl Age and Sex Identification by Means of Wing Plumage," *Special Scientific Report: Wildlife*, No. 82. (U. S. Department of the Interior, Fish and Wildlife Service.) Washington, D.C.: Government Printing Office, 1964.

Oring, L. W. "Breeding Biology and Molts of the Gadwall, *Anas strepera* Linneaus." Unpublished Ph.D. dissertation, University of Oklahoma, 1966.

Pirnie, M. D. "The Plumage Changes of Certain Waterfowl." Unpublished Ph.D. dissertation, Cornell University, 1928.

Weller, M. W. (1967). "Notes on Plumages and Weights of the Black-headed Duck, *Heteronetta atricapilla*," *Condor*, 69: 133–145.

CHAPTER 8

Evolution and Hybridization

Hinde, R. A. (1959). "Behaviour and Speciation in Birds and Lower Vertebrates," *Biological Reviews*, 34: 85–128.

Johnsgard, P. A. (1960). "Hybridization in the Anatidae and Its Taxonomic Implications," *Condor*, 62: 25–33.

———. "Behavioral Isolating Mechanisms in the Family Anatidae," in *Proceedings of the Thirteenth International Ornithological Congress*, 1963.

———. (1967). "Sympatry Changes and Hybridization Incidence in Mallards and Black Ducks," *American Midland Naturalist*, 77: 51–63.

Sharpe, R. S., and Johnsgard, P. A. (1966). "Inheritance of Behavioral Characters in F_2 Mallard x Pintail (*Anas platyrhynchos* L. x *Anas acuta* L.) Hybrids," *Behaviour*, 27: 259–272.

Sibley, C. G. (1957). "The Evolutionary and Taxonomic Significance of Sexual Dimorphism and Hybridization in Birds," *Condor*, 59: 166–191.

Yamashina, Y. (1948). "Notes on the Marianas Mallard," *Pacific Science*, 2: 121–124.

CHAPTER 9

Some Unanswered Questions

Ali, Salim, "The Pink-headed Duck," *Eleventh Annual Report of the Wildfowl Trust*. Slimbridge, England: The Wildfowl Trust, 1960.

Greenway, J. C., Jr. *Extinct and Vanishing Birds of the World*. Special Publication No. 13, American Committee for International Wild Life Protection, 1958.

Hanson, H. C. *The Giant Canada Goose*. Carbondale, Ill.: Southern Illinois University Press, 1965.

Partridge, W. H. (1956). "Notes on the Brazilian Merganser in Argentina," *Auk*, 73: 473–488.

Warner, R. E. (1963). "Recent History and Ecology of the Laysan Duck," *Condor*, 63: 3–23.

CHAPTER 10

Waterfowl, Man, and the Future

Butcher, D. *Exploring Our National Wildlife Refuges*. Boston: Houghton Mifflin, 1963.

Elder, W. H., and Woodside, D. H. "Biology and Management of the Hawaiian Goose," *Transactions of the Twenty-third North American Wildlife Conference*, 1958.

Linduska, J. P. (ed.). *Waterfowl Tomorrow*. (U. S. Department of the Interior, Bureau of Sport Fisheries and Wildlife.) Washington, D.C.: Government Printing Office, 1964.

Monnie, J. B. (1966). "Reintroduction of the Trumpeter Swan to Its Former Prairie Breeding Range," *Journal of Wildlife Management*, 30: 691–696.

Ripley, S. D. "Saving the Nene, World's Rarest Goose," *National Geographic*, November, 1965.

CHAPTER 11

IDENTIFICATION OF WATERFOWL

Broley, Jean (1950). "Identifying Nests of the Anatidae of the Canadian Prairies," *Journal of Wildlife Management*, 14: 452–456.

Robbins, C. S., Bruun, B., and Zim, H. S. *Birds of North America: A Guide to Field Identification*. New York: Golden Press, 1966.

Scott, Peter. *A Coloured Key to the Wildfowl of the World*. Slimbridge, England: The Wildfowl Trust, 1957.

Sprunt, A., IV, and Zim, H. S. *Gamebirds: A Guide to North American Species and Their Habits*. New York: Golden Press, 1961.

CHAPTER 12

MAGPIE GOOSE

Davies, S. J. J. F. (1963). "Aspects of the Behaviour of the Magpie Goose, *Anseranas semipalmata*," *Ibis*, 105: 76–98.

Frith, H. J., and Davies, S. J. J. F. (1961). "Ecology of the Magpie Goose, *Anseranas semipalmata* Latham (Anatidae)," *C.S.I.R.O. Wildlife Research*, 6: 91–141.

Johnsgard, P. A. "Breeding Biology of the Magpie Goose," *Twelfth Annual Report of the Wildfowl Trust*. Slimbridge, England: The Wildfowl Trust, 1961.

WHISTLING DUCKS

Bolen, E. G., McDaniel, B., and Cottam, C. (1964). "Natural History of the Black-bellied Tree Duck (*Dendrocygna autumnalis*) in Southern Texas," *Southwestern Naturalist*, 9: 78–88.

Dickey, D. R., and van Rossem, A. J. (1923). "The Fulvous Tree-Ducks of Buena Vista Lake," *Condor*, 25: 39–50.

Meanley, B., and Meanley, A. G. (1959). "Observations on the Fulvous Tree Duck in Louisiana," *Wilson Bulletin*, 71: 33–45.

Balham, R. W. "The Behavior of the Canada Goose (*Branta canadensis*) in Manitoba." Unpublished Ph.D. dissertation, University of Missouri, 1954.

Banko, W. E. "The Trumpeter Swan," *North American Fauna*, No. 63. (U. S. Fish and Wildlife Service.) Washington, D.C.: Government Printing Office, 1960.

Barry, T. W. (1956). "Observations on a Nesting Colony of American Brant," *Auk*, 73: 193–202.

Cooch, F. G. "The Breeding Biology and Management of the Blue Goose, *Chen caerulescens*." Unpublished Ph.D. dissertation, Cornell University, 1958.

Martin, F. W. "Behavior and Survival of Canada Geese in Utah." Bulletin 64.7. Salt Lake City, Utah State Department of Fish and Game, 1964.

Ryder, J. P. "A Preliminary Study of the Breeding Biology of Ross's Goose," *Fifteenth Annual Report of the Wildfowl Trust*. Slimbridge, England: The Wildfowl Trust, 1964.

Williams, C. W. *Honker*. Princeton, N.J.: Van Nostrand, 1967.

FRECKLED DUCK

Frith, H. J. (1965). "Ecology of the Freckled Duck, *Stictonetta naevosa* (Gould)," *C.S.I.R.O. Wildlife Research*, 10: 125–139.

Johnsgard, P. A. "Observations on Some Aberrant Australian Anatidae," *Sixteenth Annual Report of the Wildfowl Trust*. Slimbridge, England: The Wildfowl Trust, 1965.

SHELDUCKS, SHELDGEESE, STEAMER DUCKS

Hori, J. (1964). "The Breeding Biology of the Shelduck, *Tadorna tadorna*," *Ibis*, 106: 333–360.

Moynihan, M. (1958). "Notes on the Behavior of the Flying Steamer Duck," *Auk*, 75: 183–202.

Murphy, R. C. *Oceanic Birds of South America*. Vol. 1. New York: American Museum of Natural History, 1936.

Pettingill, O. S., Jr. "Kelp Geese and Flightless Steamer Ducks in the Falkland Islands," *The Living Bird, Fourth Annual Report of the Cornell Laboratory of Ornithology*, 1965.

Perching Ducks

Grice, D., and Rogers, J. P. *The Wood Duck in Massachusetts*. Boston: Massachusetts Division of Fisheries and Game, 1965.

Savage, C. *The Mandarin Duck*. London: A. & C. Black, 1952.

Stewart, P. A. "The Wood Duck, *Aix sponsa* (Linnaeus), and Its Management." Unpublished Ph.D. dissertation, Ohio State University, 1957.

Dabbling Ducks

Bennett, L. J. *The Blue-winged Teal, Its Ecology and Management*. Ames: Collegiate Press, 1938.

Gates, J. M. (1962). "Breeding Biology of the Gadwall in Northern Utah," *Wilson Bulletin*, 74: 43–67.

Johnsgard, P. A. "The Biology and Relationships of the Torrent Duck," *Seventeenth Annual Report of the Wildfowl Trust*. Slimbridge, England: The Wildfowl Trust, 1966.

Sowls, L. K. *Prairie Ducks*. Washington, D.C.: Wildlife Management Institute, 1955.

Wright, B. S. *High Tide and an East Wind: The Story of the Black Duck*. Washington, D.C.: *Wildlife Management Institute*, 1954.

Pochards

Hochbaum, H. A. *The Canvasback on a Prairie Marsh*. 2d ed. Washington, D.C.: Wildlife Management Institute, 1959.

Lokemoen, J. T. (1966). "Breeding Ecology of the Redhead Duck in Western Montana," *Journal of Wildlife Management*, 30: 668–681.

Low, J. B. (1945). "Ecology and Management of the Redhead, *Nyroca americana*, in Iowa," *Ecological Monographs*, 15: 35–69.

Mendall, H. L. (1958). "The Ring-necked Duck in the Northeast," *University of Maine Bulletin*, 60(16): 1–317.

Sea Ducks

Bengtson, Sven-Axel. "Field Studies of the Harlequin Duck in Iceland," *Seventeenth Annual Report of the Wildfowl Trust*. Slimbridge, England: The Wildfowl Trust, 1966.

Carter, B. C. "The American Goldeneye in Central New Brunswick," *Wildlife Management Bulletin*. Canadian Wildlife Service, Ser. 2, No. 9, 1958.

Cooch, F. G. (1965). "The Breeding Biology and Management of the Northern Eider (*Somateria mollissima borealis*) in the Cape Dorset Area, Northwest Territories." *Wildlife Management Bulletin*. Canadian Wildlife Service, Ser. 2, No. 10, 1965.

Gross, A. O. (1938). "Eider Ducks of Kent's Island," *Auk*, 55: 387–400.

Johnsgard, P. A. "Observations on the Breeding Biology of the Spectacled Eider," *Fifteenth Annual Report of the Wildfowl Trust*. Slimbridge, England: The Wildfowl Trust, 1964.

Rawls, C. J., Jr. "An Investigation of the Life History of the White-winged Scoter (*Melanitta fusca deglandi*)." Unpublished Master's thesis, University of Minnesota, 1949.

STIFF-TAILED DUCKS

Clark, A. (1964). "The Maccoa Duck (*Oxyura maccoa* [Eyton])," *Ostrich*, 35: 264–276.

Johnsgard, P. A. "Observations on the Behaviour and Relationships of the White-backed Duck and the Stiff-tailed Ducks," *Eighteenth Annual Report of the Wildfowl Trust*. Slimbridge, England: The Wildfowl Trust, 1967.

Low, J. B. (1941). "Nesting of the Ruddy Duck in Iowa," *Auk*, 58: 506–517.

Lowe, V. T. (1966). "Notes on the Musk Duck," *Emu*, 65: 279–290.

Weller, M. W. (1967). "Notes on Some Marsh Birds of Cape San Antonio, Argentina," *Ibis*, 109: 391–416.

Index

$\mathcal{P}$*AGE* references to topics and English vernacular names are shown in roman type; figures of photographic illustrations of species are identified by italics. Complete page references are given under species' vernacular names as summarized in chapter 12. Alternative or subspecific English names are indexed only if they actually are mentioned in the text, otherwise cross references to vernacular names used in this book are provided.